A Succession of Collections:**3**

ON THE TABLE

Mark Robbins

with an essay by Paola Antonelli

WEXNER CENTER FOR THE ARTS
The Ohio State University
Columbus, Ohio

Produced in association with the exhibition
ON THE TABLE: A SUCCESSION OF
COLLECTIONS 3
January 30–April 18, 1999
Wexner Center for the Arts
The Ohio State University
Columbus, Ohio

Organized by
MARK ROBBINS
Curator of Architecture,
Wexner Center for the Arts

A Succession of Collections *is made*
possible by a generous gift from
CHUCK AND JOYCE SHENK.

Support for this exhibition is also provided by
the Ohio Arts Council and the Wexner Center
Foundation. Promotional support is provided by
WBNS-TV.

©*1999 Wexner Center for the Arts*
The Ohio State University

Graphic Designer
JEFFREY M PACKARD

Editor
ANN BREMNER

Graduate Associate
MARIA KALINKE

Published by
WEXNER CENTER FOR THE ARTS
THE OHIO STATE UNIVERSITY
1871 North High Street
Columbus, Ohio 43210-1393

Library of Congress Catalogue Card Number:
98-89828

ISBN: 1-881390-20-9
Distributed by
DISTRIBUTED ART PUBLISHERS, NEW YORK
800-338-2665

TABLE OF CONTENTS

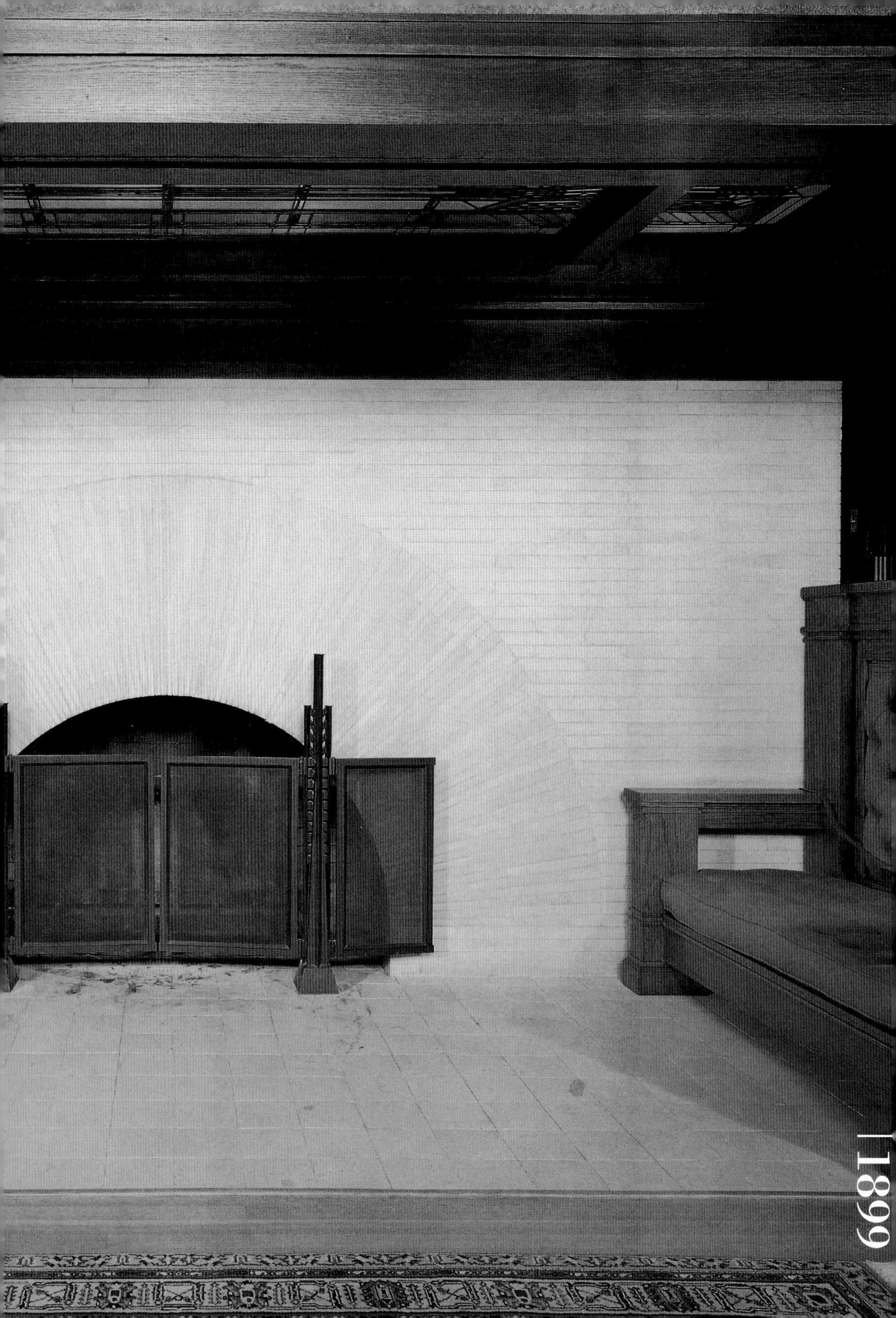
1899

FOREWORD

In its many guises—dining surface, vanity, conference prop, desk—the table is a nearly ubiquitous presence in personal, professional, and public life: the site of activities both commonplace and ceremonial. Its very familiarity makes it a provocative choice for curatorial investigation, precisely because it's so rarely examined. As the works featured in *On the Table* suggest, even an object so mundane as the table offers a wealth of insights into the evolution of design and the concept of style itself.

On the Table is the third presentation in the Wexner Center's *Succession of Collections* exhibition series, which explores significant trends, themes, genre, or historical moments along art's evolutionary path. Since the Wexner Center is not a collecting institution, these exhibitions allow us to bring together important works from major public and private collections throughout the country for the benefit of local audiences. The series provides episodic opportunities to examine the creative context from which contemporary art has emerged, while sharing with our audiences exemplary artistic resources from diverse and far-flung collections. The exhibitions in the collections series are conceived by the Wexner Center's

INTERIOR,
DANA-THOMAS HOUSE, 1899
Springfield, Illinois
Frank Lloyd Wright

Courtesy of The Illinois
Historic Preservation Agency

curatorial staff not only for their inherent interest but also for the light they shed on ideas that continue to engage artists working today.

Previous exhibitions in the series have focused on specific movements and moments in the not-too-distant history of art: abstract expressionism in *Forces of the Fifties* (1996) and surrealism in *Staging Surrealism* (1997). In *On the Table*, the temporal frame has expanded enormously, to include the nineteenth century as well as the twentieth, with a commensurate broadening of stylistic parameters. In contrast to its precursors, which both concentrated on the holdings of only a few museums, *On the Table* draws on some twenty public and private collections, each contributing one or more essential facets to this prismatic presentation.

By highlighting the multiplicity of design approaches and directions over the past two hundred years, the exhibition calls into question the strict linearity that is so often proclaimed or implied when describing our epoch's "march toward modernism." While a certain inevitability does seem to characterize the evolution of form, materials, and style from the nineteenth century to the present, it is by no means the singular path so conveniently espoused by the prevailing modernist canon. Rather, it flows like a river, with various streams and tributaries, bends and digressions, eddies and rapids—all of which make for a complex, messy, and multivalent set of currents swirling together or pulling apart. Accordingly, works in the exhibition reflect a mélange of styles: both vernacular and "high" interpretations of diverse idioms with revival modes alongside vanguard designs. By grouping the tables to encourage formal and functional comparisons rather than displaying them chronologically or in period settings, the installation reveals the flux between elaborate embellishment and spare simplicity that has marked American design throughout its history.

Ceramic tableware, which has consistently changed form along with tables, hangs on the walls of the galleries, echoing the stylistic cacophony. The inclusion of ceramics in *On the Table* also connects the center to a larger community endeavor coinciding with the exhibition. The Ohio State University and the American Ceramics Society are cohosting the annual conference of the National Council on Education for the Ceramic Arts (NCECA) in Columbus in March 1999, and the university and surrounding community are joining forces to present an extensive slate of ceramics exhibitions to coincide with the meetings. The Wexner Center is pleased to participate in this effort through the presentation of *On the Table*.

Although *On the Table* is the first Wexner Center exhibition focusing on the decorative arts, it continues a strong institutional engagement with architecture and design. Mark Robbins, curator of architecture, defined the creative premise of the exhibition and brought it to fruition with a discerning eye, a fresh (and even irreverent) perspective, and a lively appreciation for both the grand gesture and the telling detail. Mark's aesthetic and intellectual antenna have always been tuned to a rich diversity of frequencies, allowing for provocative reinterpretations of familiar patterns and signals. Paola Antonelli, the talented and dynamic associate curator in the department of architecture and design at The Museum of Modern Art, New York, complements Mark's broad view with an eloquent survey that celebrates the designers and craftsmen who fashioned American taste and stylistic sensibilities.

For this catalogue, as for its earlier sibling, *Staging Surrealism*, we have also sought to enrich the discourse by including a folio of projects by contemporary artists from many fields. The participants were invited to present—in images, words, or a combination of the two—tables of special significance to their lives. Their highly personal and memorable selections invest this publication with a particularity that inscribes "real life" into the catalogue's observation and analysis.

In the acknowledgments that conclude this book, Mark recognizes the many individuals who have contributed to the planning and realization of this exhibition and catalogue. I gratefully echo his sentiments, and would like to express special thanks to our generous lenders: the Brooklyn Museum of Art, the Henry Ford Museum & Greenfield Village, the Museum of Fine Arts, Boston, The Museum of Modern Art, New York, Musée des Arts Décoratifs de Montréal, and The Arthur E. Baggs Memorial Library Collection, The Ohio State University, as well as the individual collectors and others who have assisted us. Columbus collectors Chuck and Joyce Shenk deserve a special note of appreciation for their generous sponsorship of the *Succession of Collections* series, as do our friends at the Ohio Arts Council for their support of *On the Table* and at WBNS-TV for promotional sponsorship of this and many Wexner Center presentations. As always, I am honored to acknowledge the trustees of the Wexner Center Foundation, whose discussions and deliberations around our own board table always express a resolute commitment to this institution and its bold mission as a creative laboratory and showcase for contemporary culture in all its complex design.

Sherri Geldin
Director
WEXNER CENTER FOR THE ARTS

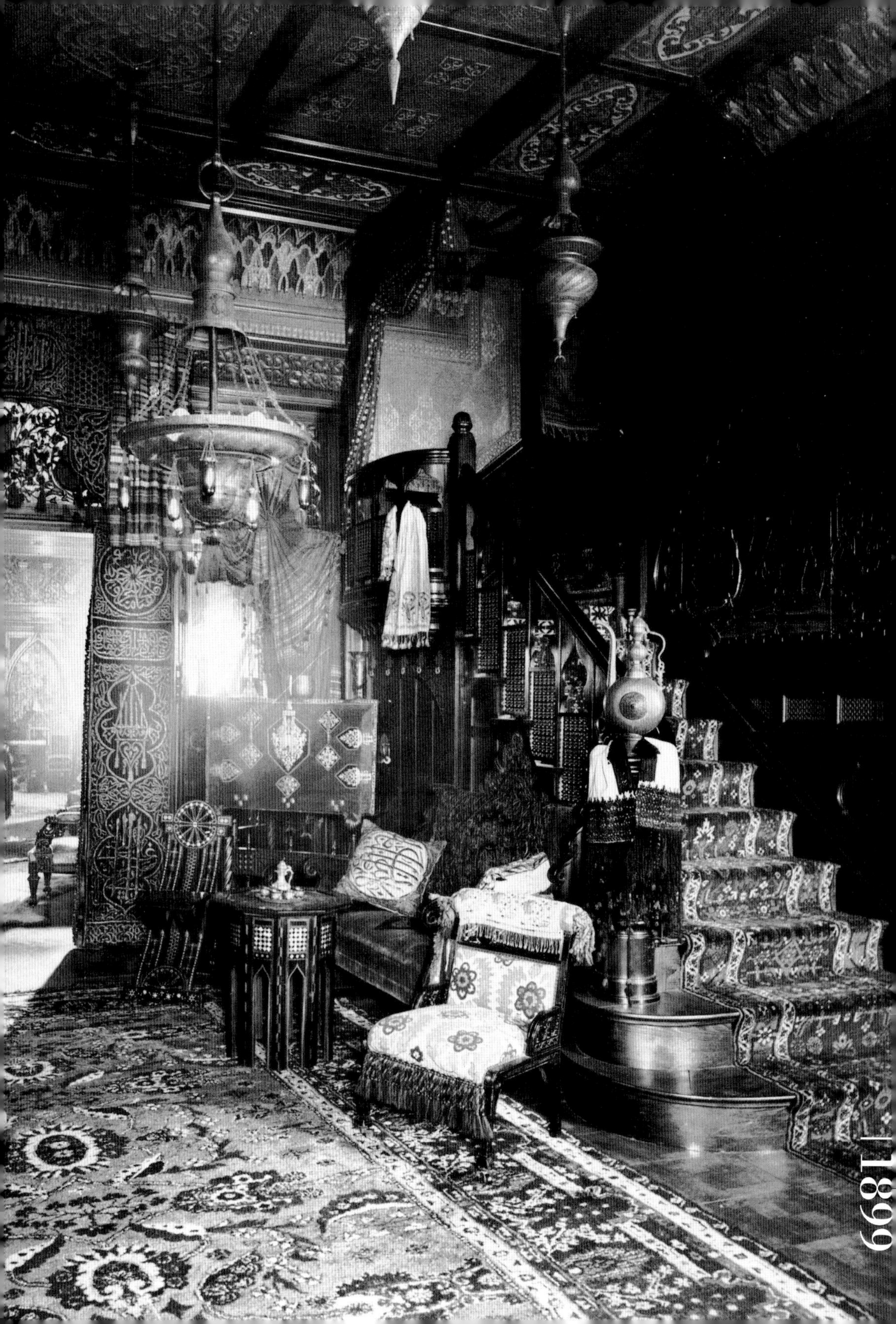
1899

FORMICA AND FALSE
CONSCIOUSNESS

MARK ROBBINS

> AS VALUES, ALL COMMODITIES ARE ONLY DEFINITE
> MASSES OF CONGEALED LABOUR-TIME. —KARL MARX[1]
>
> "HAPPINESS" IS AFTER ALL A CONSUMPTION ETHIC... —JOAN DIDION[2]

It's seemingly self-evident that the style we choose to live in reflects our backgrounds and aspirations. Décor, like fashion, represents the intersection of a host of social and economic forces: class, income, education. How we "prop" our lives—and seek guidance in, for example, the decoration, cleaning, preservation, and even scenting of our homes—reflects our anxieties and sense of propriety. Some sensibilities are local or regional in character; others are exported and consumed worldwide. Imitation is the highest form of their success, and no detail is too small to give us away.

Furniture from the old apartment in the Bronx or the rural homestead mixes with the professionally tutored selections of later affluence. Even the food—as Martha Stewart and Roland Barthes both know—reads. On a recent trip home the salad alone was a living treasury of culinary design: Hard disks of cut, peeled carrots (as opposed to julienne or lathed "baby" varieties) and bell peppers cut in

INTERIOR, HALL,
EDWARD LAUTERBACH HOUSE
2 EAST 78TH STREET, 1899
New York, New York

Museum of the City of New York;
Byron Collection

rings (as in the serving suggestions for chopped liver molds that once graced the back of Matzo boxes) no longer sat on a pale, rigid bed of iceberg leaves. Instead they accented romaine, arugula, and frisée—time marches on. Food choice and presentation have their gestalt, as do decorating touches in the home and on the table, where a similar transition was apparent. The gray and pink speckled everyday service from the sixties and the formal settings in chartreuse and rust, a wedding gift in the early fifties (now dispersed in the cupboards of the children, flamboyant survivors of mid-century American design), have been replaced with minimalist white plates used at all meals.

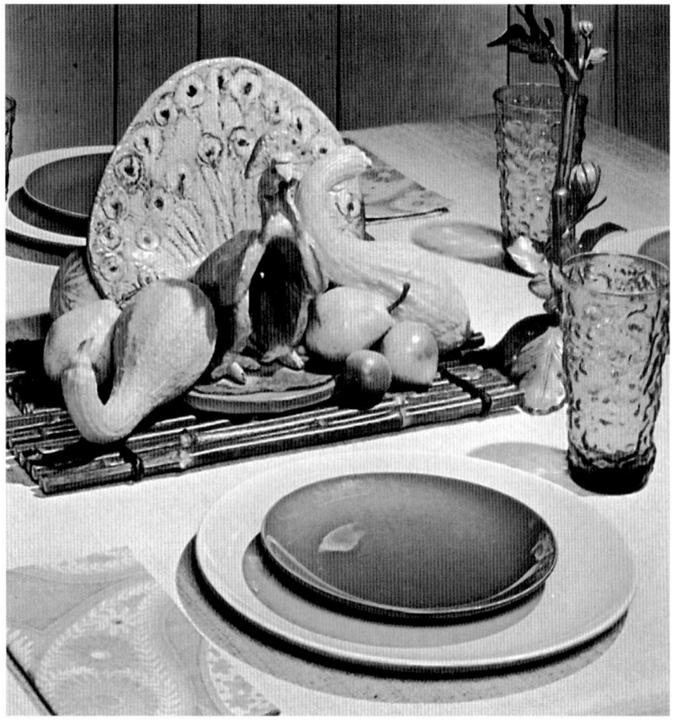

"Easter Dinner Table" from Lucy Staley,
*New Trends in Table Settings…and
Period Designs, Too*, 1968

Returning home as a visitor, like viewing other peoples' houses, reveals the scene as a field of artifacts, a local anthropology of design. Tourism depends on this avid and vicarious experience of knowing a life by seeing the place it occurred and the objects it embraced, through still lifes of tables, chairs, and beds—whether in a hacienda or Versailles or, by proxy, in the dioramas or fragments offered in museums. Our own objects and those of our time can be more difficult to see clearly. It's often only in the concentrated retro versions of the popular media that a period crystallizes so definitively as a single iconic "look."

Clearly, the evolution of form has not occurred in a single, exclusive line. Styles coexist and overlap in time and space, and cycle in and out of fashion or prominence. One can still purchase furnishings and architecture in historically based designs, as well as in the various modernisms of different decades. Economics and technology, as well as style and taste, have influenced formal vocabularies that shift between heavily ornamented and more simple, abstract forms. *On the Table* surveys these aesthetic cycles using a focused selection of tables and ceramic place settings from the nineteenth and twentieth centuries. Rather than presenting modernism as the inevitable outcome of a single path towards essential forms, the exhibition intends to tell a messier story, one that reflects the cannon of modern design mixed with elements from lesser-known sources. Drawing examples from both high and popular markets, it also demonstrates the ways in which furnishings and interiors reveal the position and aspirations of the consumer.

The exhibition places the designed object in the context of an increasingly democratized social order that has itself influenced the design of furnishings and their uses. Seventeen-piece place settings no longer are the standard, nor are expectations for specific furniture pieces for specific uses—such as tables for lady's work, dressing, or writing. This simplification in means finds parallels in the spheres of home design and fashion. The open, "casual living" plans associated with the postwar middle-class house have replaced for many the model of the grand residence with a vast number of function-specific rooms; multipurpose sportswear has supplanted requisite costumes for each activity and time of day.

The point here is to investigate the history of objects and ideas in relation to the evolution of modern design. Early in this century, architecture and design manifestoes proclaimed the desire to use design in forming a new egalitarian and modern culture. Writing in 1927, the architect Hugo Haring stated, "The present task is to create articles of use which modern man needs. We have working and sports clothes, serviceable sports equipment, serviceable tools, weapons, instruments, ships, cars—but we do not have tables, chairs, furnishings, fabrics, etc., to go with them."[3] In the U.S. too, notably in the work and writing of Frank Lloyd Wright, there was an attempt to grapple with an appropriate expression for design in the industrial age. Wright's aim was "to make of a human dwelling place a complete work of art...intimately related to modern life and fit to live in."[4]

In the writings of Adolf Loos and later of Le Corbusier, one can see an attempt to unmask the false consciousness of a culture in design terms. Both sought to retrieve the thing in its essence, designing without preconceptions or an eye towards fashion or consumer desire. Their rethinking of the problem offered an alternative to the veneer of style (as might be seen, for instance, in an Egyptian revival Bakelite radio). Loos's moral convictions are clear in his famous 1908 tract on design: "The evolution of culture is synonymous with the removal of ornament from utilitarian objects...we have fought our way through to freedom from ornament. Soon the streets of the city will glisten like white walls. Like Zion, the holy city, the capital of heaven." To Loos, ornament represented "wasted labour and ruined material."[5] Linked with the popularity of historicist revival styles, it was considered an impediment to society's progress. During the same period, however, architect Hans Polzieg wrote in a less zealous tone on the potential uses of history: "Flight from everything historical can no more bring salvation than a purely decorative return to forms from the past."[6]

Beyond questions of historicism, however, there is at issue the persistent equation between value and technical skill, which is apparent in ornament, surface treatments, and virtuosic forms. Objects of fine and applied art manifested the time invested: labor crystallized in the service of ecclesiastical or secular wealth. Complex works of art and architecture honored their owners, with intricacy and scale intended to produced awe and wonder. In a Marxist reading, these works represent excess capital turned into the luxury of nonessential craft. A sod house, log cabin, or barn expresses an economy of limited means. No expenditure, in money, materials, or physical energy, is in excess. As in the purity of engineered objects or the functionalism of wartime construction, form is derived from necessity. Appliquéd ornamentation, by contrast, expresses a desire to show excess. Surface can be seen as a subtext in veneer, in materials and their imitations.

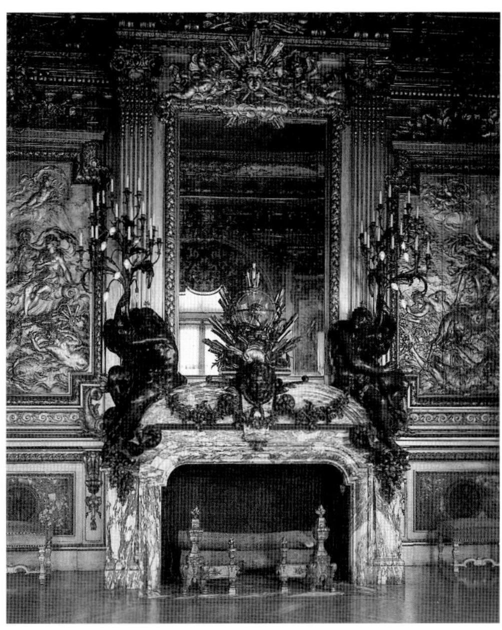

Ballroom Fireplace, Marble House, 1888–1892
Newport, Rhode Island

Extravagance is predicated on the choice and ability to display grandly. In America this flowered in the late nineteenth century through social as well as technological developments, which had also helped produce a broad consuming middle class. As Siegfried Giedion says in his remarkable history of mechanization, this period "meant the rule of pseudo monumentality...This same orientation was responsible for the furniture of the ruling taste, with its excess of decoration and ornamentation. Things that only the topmost classes had been able to purchase, mechanization now made possible."[7]

The era in the U.S. was characterized by this multiplication of styles, a "rampant eclecticism."[8] The strand of houses in Newport, for example, demonstrated the power of newly wealthy industrialists and entrepreneurs. A proliferation of rooms and styles mimicked with great precision the materials and spaces of renaissance or baroque palaces. Exclusive and complex sets of rituals and behavior formed an elaborate social counterpart. Rooms were made for all uses and classes of people: parlors for men and women, servants' wings, libraries, billiard rooms. The furnishings and architecture were really as much about display as accommodation. This accumulation of goods and appropriation of past styles set standards for future emulation across classes.

While façades with classical orders in limestone were applied to country estates and urban mansions, mass-produced façades of brownstone simulated wealth on tenements. Cast iron façades were shipped in components as far as Alaska and tacked onto wood frames. Industrial, commercial, and frontier streets were laminated in renaissance layers. Other production techniques, like lathing, made the gingerbread and hyperbolic wooden ornament of American Victorian possible. The presence of historical forms signaled solid social standing; parlor doors with etched glass and Gothic borders divided rooms in the overcrowded railroad flats of an aspiring late-nineteenth-century working class.

One hundred years later the American home front has become an intensively marketed terrain. Although incursions of modern open plans have occurred, the proliferation of room types and styles continues as a popular goal, a carryover from Newport and the country estate. (One Connecticut architect has developed a lexicon of terms to satisfy her clients' expansive plans. Labels on drawings include "Her study," "Wrapping Room," and "Commons,"[9] which take their place beside the more pedestrian real estate lingo of "Family," "Florida," and "Great" rooms.) For most households, approaching such elaboration means shopping at huge retail malls for construction supplies and décor: from Target and K-Mart to Ikea. At high and low ends fashion names like Polo and Prada are invoked in the service of matching linens and moldings. They offer visions of good taste at all price points. This stylistic abundance is made possible through techniques of modern production, marketing, and distribution. In this mix, modernism is one style among many—and one only sporadically embraced by a wide public.

According to historian Adrian Forty, "The success of capitalism has always depended upon its capacity to innovate and sell new products. Yet, paradoxically, most societies in which capitalism has taken hold have expressed resistance to the newness of things."[10] The difficulty encountered with universal, or even broad-based, acceptance of the new in design sprang, at least in part, from the residual desires for objects associated with traditional versions of high style. Though the sleek abstraction of modernism may have been valued within limited sectors of the market, its association with a known lineage was by and large mute. It remains a high style, getting into most homes in recent decades only through a coffee maker, food processor, or large screen TV.

Unfamiliar technology, for example, was long clad in familiar materials, domesticating devices for the home market by inscribing them into a known past. The wood grain on stereos referred back to the cabinets of the gramophone, which did require wood as a sounding box. The earliest radios also had massive wooden cabinets to harmonize with home décor in renaissance, Gothic, or other revival styles. Televisions followed suit, appearing in a variety of historical garbs. Wood, even if unrelated to function, as in the side panels of a Vista Cruiser, continues to evoke often forgotten origins.

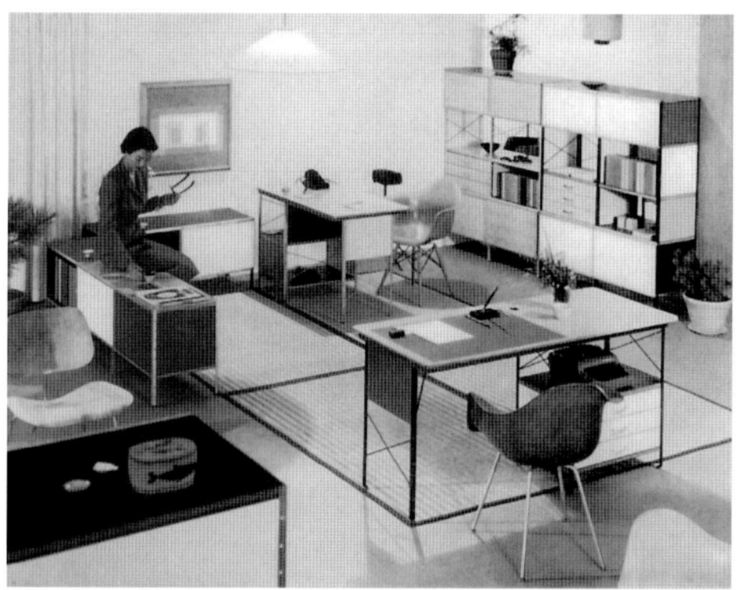

Eames Storage Units/Desks from
The Herman Miller Collection (catalogue), 1952

In the postwar era some of the modern aesthetic did take hold in the popular mind through television, worlds fairs, and dancing appliance ads. But rarely did the average home and its furnishings epitomize that world of the future. To the majority of consumers the unornamented interior and exterior surfaces of modern architecture and design still appear barren and alien. Ersatz finishes endure in white French provincial bedroom suites and Florentine settees. Talk shows headline hot tubs, screening rooms, and spiral stairs to signify the homes of the stars. Similarly, crowds at popular home shows ogle triple ellipse Corian sink tops and symmetrically placed, built-in, his-and-hers hair dryers ensconced in library paneling of pressed wood. Beyond the vastness of the space and the number of rooms, it's not the quality of appointments and furnishings but the overall excess that marks these homes as consumer paragons. Surfaces and accoutrements—not spatial invention or imaginative design—convey the appearance of worth.

The tables and ceramic place settings exhibited in *On the Table* have been selected in order to suggest the complexity of modernism's development. Dating from 1800 to 1998, they range from Shaker pieces to contemporary furniture designs and from the Reagan presidential china to melamine plates. Looking at these works offers multiple ways to survey a history of American design. One could trace differing production techniques. From early hand crafting to complete industrial production, workshops involving master craftsmen and assistants yielded to individual designers employed by large manufacturing firms bent on capturing a mass market in the postwar years. One could also study the evolution of materials and techniques or outline the economic standing of the nation and its population. Changes in social mores have obviated the need for certain types of furnishings and established the necessity of others. Such shifts have had an impact on the forms produced.

While showing a history of styles and techniques, these pieces are also a record of the work of a series of furniture and ceramic designers, artists, and architects. Although many of the works are by well-known figures and associated with a standard history of modern design, others are by less-known or anonymous designers. The intent is to present often disparate objects that for varying reasons share some resemblance.

The objects are grouped to spur associations—connected in terms of either function or form—and assembled in the gallery to encourage viewer interaction, drawing from and revising the traditions of period room displays. The tables are set on low pedestals arranged in a grid reminiscent of urban blocks, with the ceramics hung in constellations on the walls. Viewers navigate through the non-chronological field of tables with objects positioned at eye level; dates of the work in large typescript form a pattern of subtitles on the sides of the bases. Five photomurals of American interiors provide backdrops that bracket the display. Paired modern and historically based interiors from the 1890s and the 1990s flank an iconic image of a mid-century modern room. Thematically, the images underscore the point that the simplified, abstracted planes associated with modern design have been available alongside historical styles throughout the twentieth century. The popularity of different styles and the waves between ornamentation and simplicity represent not so much availability and the design trajectory of modernism as the desire of the consumer. These objects have "varied in appearance, not because of the immorality or willfulness of their makers, but because of the circumstances of their production and consumption."[11]

The table was chosen as the central object for the exhibition in part because of its variety and familiarity. It reflects or responds to consumer needs and desires, just as houses do—but at a smaller scale—and has possible associations with specific gender, culture, and class identities. Beyond its basic property as a plane raised above the ground, the table enforces a specific posture for the body at rest and performing tasks through its form and height. It defines the geography of specific points in a room and has changed in scale, form, and function in response to changes in the architecture that houses it and the work and leisure activities of those who use it. At fast food restaurants, for instance, economy, public hygiene, and maintenance determine the form of the fluorescent laminate table, with suspended seating welded to its pedestal. The dinette is going the way of the davenport, but coffee tables are now marketed for the rotating storage of CDs.[12]

The table is also of interest because of its position as the site of ritual activities: from dining to applying make-up, it is a stage. The spatial relations of the dining table, for instance, make clear the formal relations between persons. The salt salver was once set at the head of the table. The valuable commodity and its control conferred status. The boardroom is also laid out with a clear hierarchy,

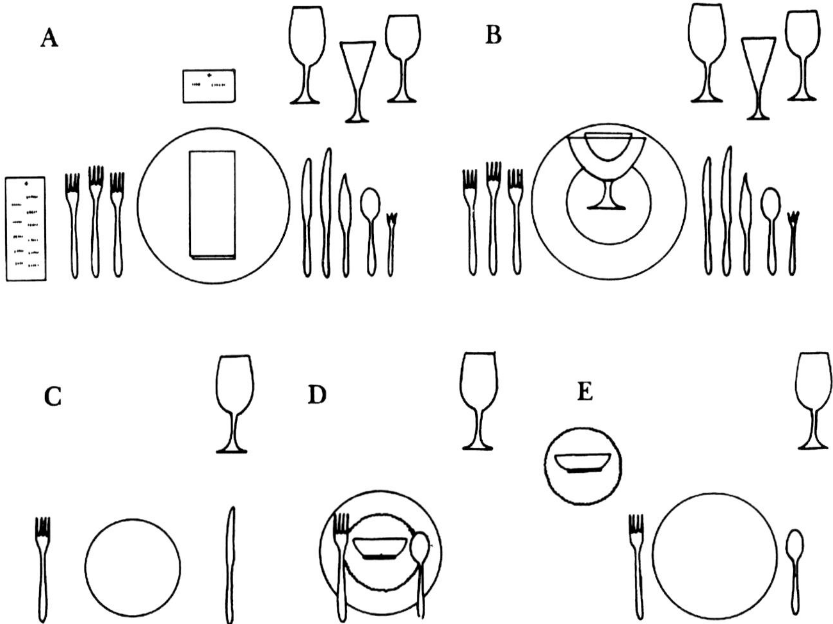

FORMAL DINNER. (A) In holders, place card above plate; menu card left. Water and two wine glasses in place. *1st course* (B): (Small spoon replaces oyster fork if fruit or melon served.) Wine glasses removed as used; water glass remains. *2nd course*: Soup plate set on service plate after 1st course plate and silver removed. *3rd course*: Remove soup on soup plate, service plate and silver removed; entree (creamed sweetbreads, timbales, etc.) served on plate. Entree plate and fork removed. *4th course*: Roast served on large dinner plate. *5th course* (C): Salad served on chilled plate; plate and silver smaller than for meat course. *6th course* (D): Setting cleared except for water glasses. Table crumbed. Dessert plate and silver brought in; finger bowl with doily may come in on dessert plate. Guest moves doily and plate to left (E); dessert now served. *7th course*: Coffee served away from table. (If served at table, cup, saucer and silver brought in after dessert.)

Illustration and text from Lucy Staley,
*New Trends in Table Settings...and
Period Designs, Too*, 1968

recalling the endless debate on the shape of the table for the Paris peace talks. The symbolic importance of position in relation to the preferred axis makes geometry and proximity charged coordinates.

The wedding is one of the last vestiges of formal dining in American culture. Perhaps the misty approximation of a palmier era of entitlement, permitting some level of elaboration in costume and hosting, accounts for the continuing fascination with a spectacular, short-lived investment. The theatricality of the event requires a complexity in table service and décor not unlike the banquets of Victorian America. It is a remnant of a social and economic structure that also faded between the wars; one that had allowed for and required an intensive service economy.

Many paths are discernible in the development of design, but, as in any history, one asserts itself most forcefully or gains the historical imprimatur as the spirit of the age. Style can evolve from above and below and Hollywood helps in the homogenization, as do television and magazines, insuring a generally democratic dispersion. Even with assumptions about an internationalization of style, however, appeal remains wildly local. Objects represent how we think we would like to be portrayed, as well as what we need and can afford. Taste may be so problematic because it is a luxury item—the luxe of discretion, choice.

1. Karl Marx, "The Critique of Capitalism," in *The Marx-Engels Reader,* edited by Robert E. Tucker (New York: W. W. Norton & Company, 1972), p. 203.

2. Joan Didion, *After Henry* (New York: Vintage Books, 1993), p. 210.

3. Hugo Haring, "Formulations toward a Reorientation in the Applied Arts" (1927), in *Programs and Manifestoes on 20th-Century Architecture,* edited by Ulrich Conrads, translated by Michael Bullock (Cambridge, MA: MIT Press, 1975), p. 105.

4. Frank Lloyd Wright, "Organic Architecture" (1910), in *Programs and Manifestoes on 20th-Century Architecture,* p. 25.

5. Adolf Loos, "Ornament and Crime" (1908), in *Programs and Manifestoes on 20th-Century Architecture,* pp. 19; 23.

6. Hans Polzieg, "Fermentation in Architecture" (1906), in *Programs and Manifestoes on 20th-Century Architecture,* p. 15.

7. Siegfried Giedion, *Mechanization Takes Command: A Contribution to Anonymous History* (New York: Oxford University Press, 1948), p. 395.

8. Jonathan M. Woodham, *Twentieth-Century Ornament* (New York: Rizzoli, 1990), p. 27.

9. The architect is Jeanne Stoney, Austin Patterson Disston, Architects.

10. Adrian Forty, *Objects of Desire: Design and Society 1750–1980* (New York, Pantheon Books, 1986), p. 11.

11. Ibid., p. 13.

12. Examples include the *Charlotte* and *Marvin* coffee tables designed by Andy Hope of Co-Motion Design, San Francisco.

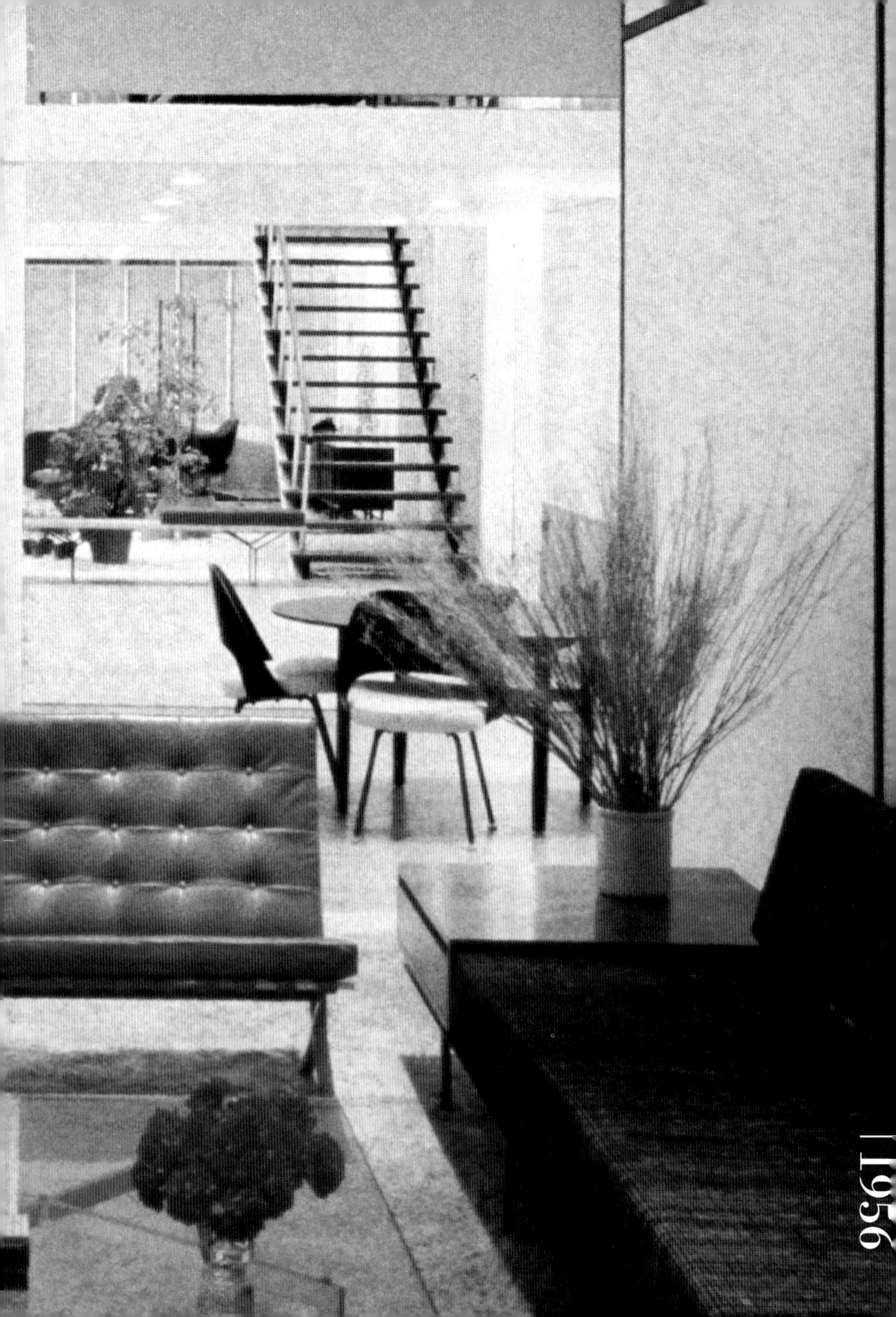

1956

Paola Antonelli

Tables are omnipresent in the history of Western design, so much that they can be used as keys to an extended narration of its events. They can be pinpointed as symbols of historical moments in the evolution of society and evaluated in their capacity to fully represent their times. The tables and tabletop objects in this particular exhibition can be considered main witnesses in the development of American material culture, as they comment on design and technology, on the vagaries of taste, on the evolution of materials, and on the timely paragons of comfort and availability. They bespeak the search for an American style and for American society's identity. The subject of this exhibition is not simply tables and design, as it might appear, but rather the presence of recurring and contrasting ideals in the American domestic environment, and the way American craftsmen and designers interpreted and guided them.

To convey the subject's loaded presence in the most effective way, the curator has chosen to display only the tables and their paraphernalia, which often represent a family's most direct statement about taste and social status. By disregarding chairs, and by focusing not simply on a typological area—tables—but

San Francisco Showroom
of Knoll, Inc., 1956

Courtesy of Knoll, Inc.

rather on a geographic region—the table milieu—of everyday design, he has established a meaningful level of abstraction that conveys a strong critical viewpoint and that can be approached from different thresholds. This essay is about the people that were not around, but rather behind, the tables: the designers and craftsmen that actualized those ideals and offered them to the world. In particular, its content highlights the progressive definition in the forties and fifties of the American approach to design, an original and stereotypical paradigm that lists among its components a taste for logical and economical beauty, a democratic view of art applied to mass-production, a mighty faith in technology and in the future, and an unmistakable drive towards simplification and rationalization.

American designers have been strong forces behind the evolution of society, and even in their designs for tables, they have often embraced social needs and economic considerations. The path towards a true American design was nonetheless long. At the beginning of the nineteenth century, America was still, psychologically, a European colony. American society strove to emulate the refinement of European aristocracy. The furniture for the wealthy was thus generally imported; the middle class longed for the same ideal of luxury and style—and bought imitations. A few emigrant craftsmen, such as Benjamin Henry Latrobe from England and Pierre Charles L'Enfant from France, had brought with them many neoclassic models for everybody to copy, along with detailed pattern books. The American craftsmen provided furnishings that often mimicked the foreign elegance of their European counterparts, as exemplified by the delightful woman's work table that is the oldest work in the exhibition. Its pleated bag of blue silk recalls the high-waisted dresses worn by courtesans in Napoleon's neoclassic empire. Style after style, Gothic revival after neoclassicism, Eurocentrism continued throughout the century, as exemplified by several tables in the exhibition, in particular émigré Leon Marcotte's grandiose inlaid table, the peculiar "Rustic Table" of painted twigs, and the complex Parker brass table.

Even though most American craftsmen did not seem preoccupied with finding their own voice, the American products exhibited at the London Exposition of 1851 were criticized for being too austere and lacking ornamentation. Somehow, America's true inspiration—essentiality—was starting to permeate its material culture, albeit still undercover. One of its best exemplars, Shaker furniture, had existed since the eighteenth century. In the introduction to their *Shaker Built*, Paul Rocheleau and June Sprigg state: "The Shakers' attitude towards their buildings was no more sentimental than their attitude about their own flesh-and-blood bodies. It was the spirit of usefulness within that mattered, not the vessel itself."[1] The Shakers can be considered one of the first examples not only of the American Arts and Crafts movement, but also of American modern design.

Shaker furnishings and interior architecture displayed a sobriety and honesty that were a direct portrayal of the circumstances that generated them. The available materials were used in harmony with their capabilities, according to what Arthur Pulos calls "the principle of beauty as the natural by-product of functional refinement,"[2] a principle that will also be recalled by many in this century to define design excellence. Any detail in the minimal Shaker furnishings was dictated by a practical purpose, and the furnishings belonged to a general design plan that rationalized the domestic space. Even though the Shakers' designs did not seem to be much appreciated by the general public, echoes of their philosophy can be found in revolutionary proposals destined for the mainstream. The Beecher sisters, for instance, preached in 1869 in favor of a more rational domestic envi-

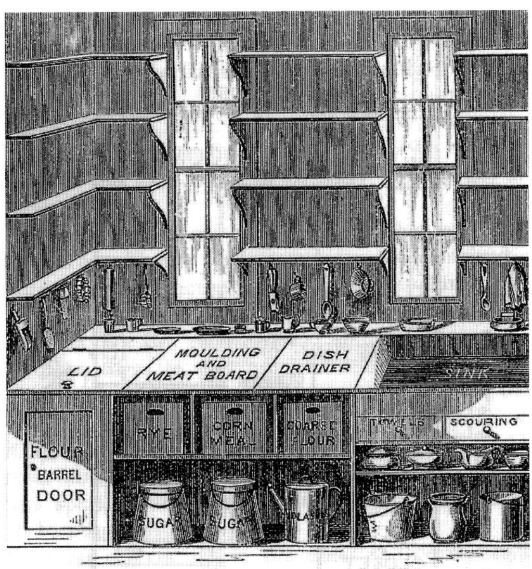

Kitchen plan from Catherine E. Beecher
and Harriet Beecher Stowe, *The American
Woman's Home*, 1869

ronment, designed to provide "modes of economising time, labor, and expense by the close packing of conveniences" so that "small and economical houses can be made to secure most of the comforts and many of the refinements of large and expensive ones."[3] Their positive moralism and confidence in democracy can be found in other small local phenomena, like Rookwood Pottery, a company established in 1880 in Cincinnati, Ohio, to provide a respectable source of employment for women.

The search for simplicity continued. At the beginning of the century, many—among them Louis Comfort Tiffany and Gustav Stickley—praised the qualities of taste and simplicity as opposed to vulgarity and redundancy. The introduction of electricity provided new domestic comforts as well as a new visual model of inspiration, the machine, which was celebrated in the first decades of the century by such independent design professionals as Raymond Loewy, John Vassos, Walter Dorwin Teague, Kem Weber, and Norman Bel Geddes. It is at this time that American design was first described as "modern." The Depression of the thirties pushed the search for alternative materials even farther, moved the whole world of design towards a more economical perspective, and helped Americans find and recognize the value of their own national design. Aluminum, chrome plating, plastics, and all the other materials suitable for mass-production did not, in fact, allow for much decorative detailing. On the other hand, these materials provided American designers with new expressive possibilities, ranging from art deco and streamline styles to functionalism. Two tables in the exhibition, Kem Weber's vanity and Gilbert Rohde's desk, both from 1934 and both made of steel, are examples of different responses to the same inspiration, interestingly juxtaposing not only European and American sources, but also West and East coasts.

Born in Berlin, Kem Weber was stranded in the United States by World War I while making a business trip in 1913. He established himself in Hollywood and became a dramatic interpreter of the Machine Age theme. Gilbert Rohde, born and raised in the United States, was trained as a design professional and in 1935 became the director of the Design Laboratory in New York, a school that was meant to be the American Bauhaus. Several companies based in the Midwest, where the real mass-production was happening, used Rohde's professional services. Among them were Heywood-Wakefield (with a major plant in Chicago) and Herman Miller (headquartered in Zeeland, Michigan). In the mid-thirties, he designed a line of furniture in tubular steel for the Troy Sunshade Company of Troy, Ohio, including the Rohde desk in the exhibition. Weber's vanity is an aesthetic exploration in

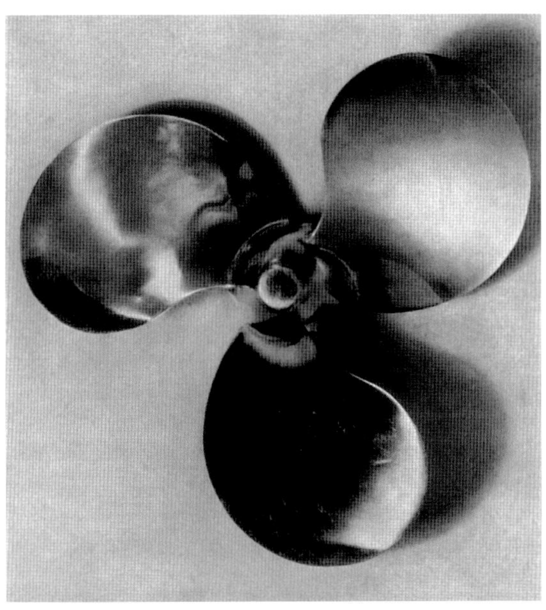

Outboard Propeller, Aluminum Company of America
Plate 41 from The Museum of Modern Art's
Machine Art exhibition catalogue, 1934

art deco style; Rohde's desk, an American variation on the European theme of tubular steel furniture, displays attention to technology and mass production. Formal investigation is not sacrificed but set within the limits of the manufacturing process, in a true expression of industrial design philosophy.

The importance of the machine was interpreted by some as an aesthetic discovery, even more surprising because it celebrated pure, untamed functionality. In the famous *Machine Art* show at the Museum of Modern Art in New York in 1934, Philip Johnson honored the platonic beauty of coils, propeller blades, and other objects meant to do nothing else than function with precision. The Age of the Machine inspired some mainstream designers to produce new, almost mythological shapes. The manner called streamline came from observing abstract engineered forms for industrial production and was a dramatic symbolization of America's present and future. Oddly mixed with an organic and biomorphic sensitivity, it became in the 1930s the national style for everyday objects, such as cars, typewriters, and vacuum cleaners. Furniture generally escaped its influence, with the exception of the famous Airline armchair by Kem Weber and of the aluminum table by Frederick Kiesler also featured in this exhibition. In the galleries of MoMA, the Kiesler table sits next to a Hobart meat-slicer, its contemporary, and the two objects curiously echo each other. One of the most renowned examples of streamline is the American Modern dinnerware by Russel Wright.

Russel Wright's work exemplifies the Depression's positive effects on industrial design and the pragmatic optimism that followed. Wright, who devoted his career to "humanizing functional design"[4] and elevating mass-production, applied himself to studying new materials and manufacturing processes and focused his attention on standardization and availability. At the beginning of the thirties, he had already worked on an affordable line of housewares and hospitality items in spun aluminum, and he had developed a Scandinavian-looking line of furniture in solid bleached maple. The American Modern line of ceramic dinnerware, introduced in 1939, has become an icon of modernist design. Although highly decorative because of their soft shapes and soft colors, the items in the line were nonetheless strictly functional, and their round, undecorated forms were direct consequences of the manufacturing process.

Eva Zeisel, an illustrious immigrant from Hungary, is Wright's interesting counterpart in this narration. Her work and Wright's appear similar on superficial consideration but reflect different motivations and processes. Zeisel, who arrived in the United States at the end of the thirties after having being imprisoned in the Soviet Union during Stalin's purges, brought with her the best of European intellectual craftsmanship. A ceramist trained in the workshops of Eastern Europe, she had worked with Nikolai Suetin, absorbed the new trends toward organic forms, and developed her own position in opposition to that of the Bauhaus. Her work with Castleton China, a manufacturer based in New Castle, Pennsylvania, was groundbreaking more for its formal research than its impact on the American market. Her *Museum* dinnerware of 1942–45, presented at the Museum of Modern Art, represents one of the purest peaks of high-end organic design—as well as the American elite's continuing veneration for models imported from abroad.

In 1947, the Museum of Modern Art launched a competition for "Low-Cost Furniture Design" intended to boost the production of low-cost, mass-produced home furnishings with an eye to "the national economy and the general welfare of the peoples of all countries," as the catalogue reports. The goal was to build a better society and better lives after the long wartime years, and designers were considered to be instrumental in this effort to improve the environment. In the museum's ideal, the newly designed furniture was supposed to reflect the social, economic, technological, and aesthetic tendencies of the time and to be geared towards innovation. Charles and Ray Eames received second prize.[5]

The most fascinating team in design history, Charles and Ray Eames were unique in their ability to represent the common man in any object that they designed. Their partnership brought about a new and constructive solidarity between art, science, and design, and made them available to the masses. The Eameses exemplified the most original American path to modernism. The trademark European modernism of the 1930s relied heavily on ideology; West Coast modernism, based on a straightforward and optimistic reality, was the champion of American sensibility and idealism. This new architecture "for modern living" established itself after World War II as a way to represent and accommodate the booming middle class in an innovative residential model, all the while using materials and techniques made available by the now-idle war industries based in the area. The Californian approach to design and architecture was about practice, not about theory, and it required that homes be comfortable and efficient, both in the way they were used and in the way they were built. Utility became the guiding principle and the key to a new aesthetic, which became the official American "good taste," a taste that was born out of economy.

Charles and Ray Eames fit comfortably into this spirit. All their production apparently stemmed from necessity. The Eameses' furnishings are an outstanding contribution towards an autonomous American kind of architecture and design, and their influence can be measured to this day in the self-confident design method used by several professionals. With their universal and original language they were able to give the world, especially the American world, a body of useful neologisms to build on. Particularly interesting was their collaboration with George Nelson, who succeeded Gilbert Rohde as the director of design at Herman Miller from 1946 to 1965. Nelson, the designer of such icons as the Marshmallow sofa, was responsible for gathering the outstanding club of American designers around the company, including Alexander Girard and Isamu Noguchi, as well as the Eameses. He represented a new generation of design visionaries that advocated against commercialism and rather condensed the essence of American design into a new idea of domestic and office comfort.

Knoll, established by Hans Knoll in 1938, was also among the companies that pursued high design for mass production. And Knoll similarly gathered around himself a distinguished design group, which included Eero Saarinen and Harry Bertoia among others. Richard Schultz joined Knoll's Design/Development group in 1951, appointed by Hans Knoll himself because of Schultz's innate ability to transform sculptural form into manageable and affordable objects, the basis of the Knoll philosophy. He worked at first with Harry Bertoia, then developed the Petal table that represents him in the exhibition.

In the manufacturing plants of the Midwest, American design had found its true modern voice, which continued when modernism was threatened worldwide in the sixties. In the course of this century in the Western world, the rules and regulations of the modern movement, set in the 1920s and 1930s, have become the point of reference for all architecture and design, both produced and conceived. Though a "modern" attitude, identified by the search for an objective approach to designing and building, has always existed, its deliberate formulation by the Bauhaus and such masters as Gropius, Le Corbusier, and Mies van der Rohe has elevated it to a moral and aesthetic principle, to a powerful, transnational dogma. After the first revolutionary explosion, however, modernism became a formal imposition, and local cultures have proved to be the safest and most efficient way to rebel against modernism without giving up the great qualities of modern design. In the United States, the country of cultural pluralism, this contingency generated many diverse responses, exemplified in this exhibition by Robert Venturi's table. This object draws inspiration from quintessential American phenomena, such as pop art and Las Vegas.

In the last decades, America for a while turned again to Europe for style paradigms, while looking for a personal, polyphonic way to interpret the postindustrial era. The late 1990s, on the other hand, are peculiarly similar to the second postwar period. These are spiritual times, marked by renewed attention devoted to domestic living and fueled by concerns about the environment and a strong political consciousness worldwide. Design trends are often accurate reflections of social change, and the economy and sensibility that envelop the world today, after an age of excess, are very strong forces indeed. Morality, sometimes even moralism, is a recognizable feature of many contemporary objects, and so is curiosity: about materials, processes, and functions. In the mean time, many new, customizable, mutant materials have become available, some by the natural evolution of research, some by the end of the Cold War. All in all, contemporary American design is frequently experimental in its use of materials and often inspired by genuine necessity. Even so, it sustains elements of surprise and deep intellectual beauty because it relies more on invention and reduction than on the elaboration of previous styles.

The exhibition is rich with examples of contemporary American design's stylistic eclecticism and material skills. The trend is based today on experimentation on the single object, and American design is experiencing a renaissance worldwide. Many young professionals, such as Karim Rashid, Maya Lin, and Ali Tayar, have become renowned interpreters of contemporary times. The best contemporary objects are those whose presence expresses history and contemporaneity; those that exude humors of the material culture that generated them, while at the same time speaking a global language; those that carry both memory and insight into the future; those that spark a sense of belonging—in the world, in these exciting times of cultural and technical possibilities. The best contemporary American design expresses consciousness and an interesting rejection of style in favor of a presence that stems from within the design process.

PAOLA ANTONELLI is Associate Curator in the Department of Architecture and Design at The Museum of Modern Art, New York. She has been a contributing editor for *Domus* and design editor for *Abitare* and has contributed articles to *Graphis, I.D., Metropolis,* and *Metropolitan Home.* Her exhibitions for MOMA include *Mutant Materials in Contemporary Design* (1995), and she has also taught and lectured on design, design history, and architecture.

1. Paul Rocheleau and June Sprigg, *Shaker Built* (New York: The Monacelli Press, 1994), p. 10.

2. Arthur J. Pulos, *American Design Ethic* (Cambridge, MA: MIT Press, 1983), p. 7.

3. Catherine Beecher and Harriet Beecher Stowe, *The American Woman's Home* (New York: J. B. Ford, 1869), quoted in Pulos, p. 172.

4. Interview with Russel Wright, Pulos, p. 292.

5. The Eameses' award was for a chair credited to Charles Eames and the University of California at Los Angeles. The first place award was shared by Don R. Knorr of San Francisco and George Leowald of Berlin-Frohnau. The Eameses shared the second place award with Davis J. Pratt of Chicago. Edgar Kaufmann, Jr., *Prize Designs for Modern Furniture from the International Competition for Low-Cost Furniture Design* (New York: The Museum of Modern Art, 1950).

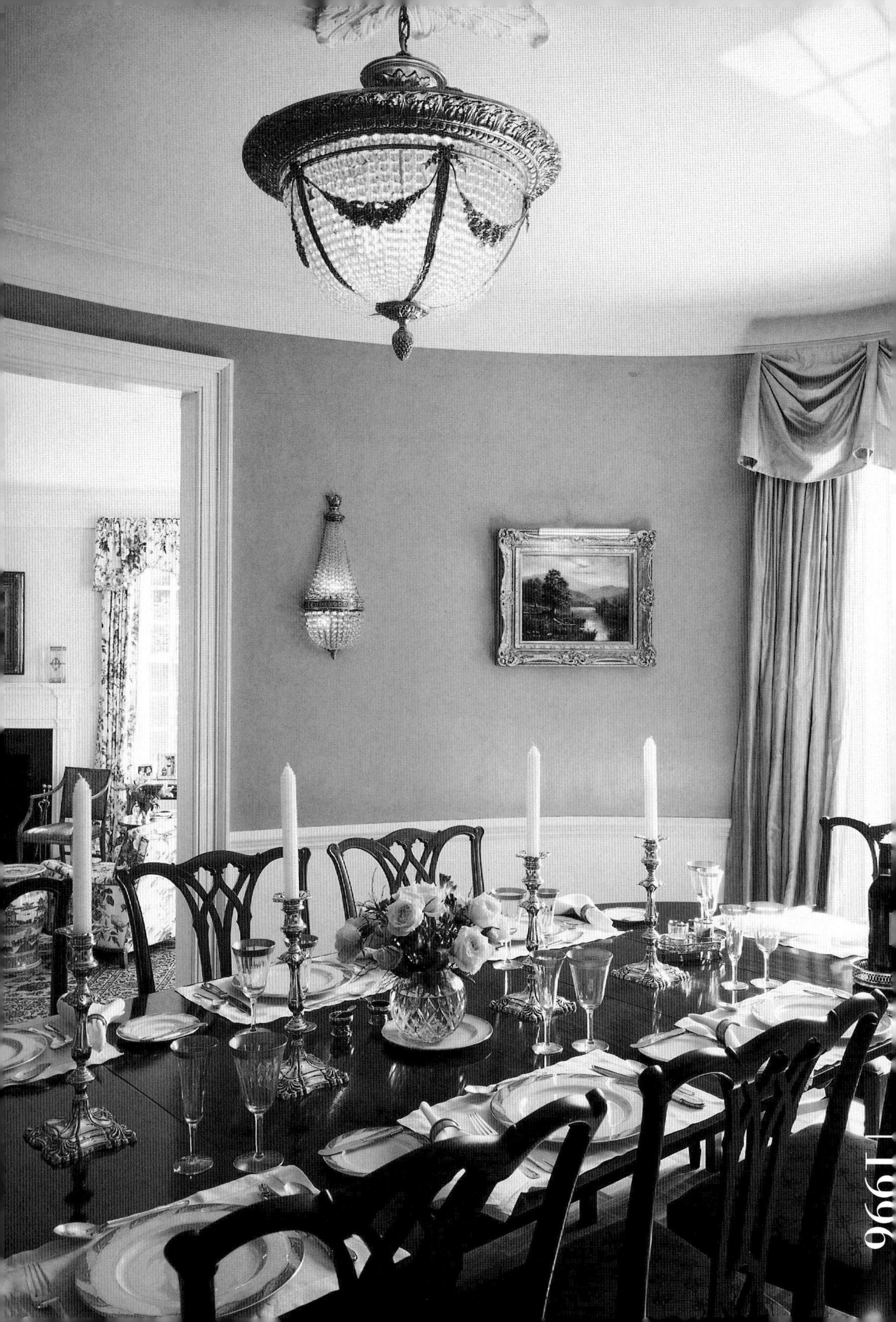

These groups reflect some of
the thematic connections highlighted
in the installation of the exhibition.

GEORGIAN OVAL DINING ROOM, 1996
Greenwich, Connecticut
Austin Patterson Disston Architects, LLC

Courtesy of Austin Patterson
Disston Architects, LLC

The table by Leon Marcotte, the most elaborate in the exhibition, is in the Louis XVI revival style.[1] Originally from France, Marcotte was among the most notable émigré cabinetmakers working in New York in the mid-1800s, and his work reveals how sophisticated furniture makers in large U.S. cities had become by mid-century. Made of ebonized wood with figural ormolu mounts and brass inlay, the table takes the form of a piece that might have been used in a European court and is a high example of the eclecticism popular in grand homes of the time. The anonymous folk table of painted twigs reflects the revival of another style that had originated in the eighteenth century: a "rustic" version of rococo. This romantic antidote to high court sensibility became popular again with the rococo revival of the 1850s. Spurred by the vogue for Adirondack camps, rustic styles flourished in the 1880s and remained popular into the 1930s. The brass table by the Charles Parker Company is in yet another revival style, Gothic, rendered here in interchangeable metal components.

It treats these machined and turned pieces in the geometricized "Reform Gothic" manner then fashionable in Europe and the U.S. The ornament is flattened, achieved through piercing rather than carving, with scrollwork and applied detail. The simplification of detail suits the material and production requirements.

The transformations of ornamental styles in these works prefigure the postmodern reuse of historical elements seen in Robert Venturi's cabriole leg table of 1984. Venturi, an architect associated with the reintegration of historical forms in design, uses the form of the cabriole leg, which dates to the seventeenth century in Europe, and reduces it to profile. He manipulates the point of view in an almost cubist manner, rotating the legs so that three are always visible in profile and the fourth is seen only as a thin black edge. Surface ornament here is reduced to a busy laminate pattern also designed by the architect, one of the finishes available from the manufacturer.

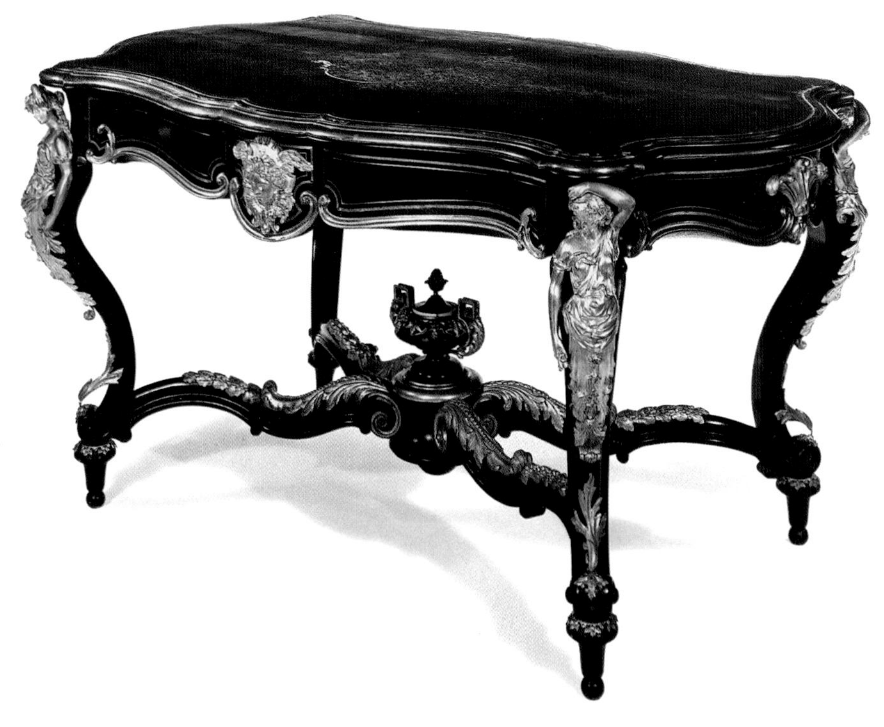

TABLE, C. 1865
Leon Marcotte
Ebonized woods, brass, and gilded metal
30½ x 57½ x 37½ in.

Brooklyn Museum of Art;
Gift of the Roebling Society

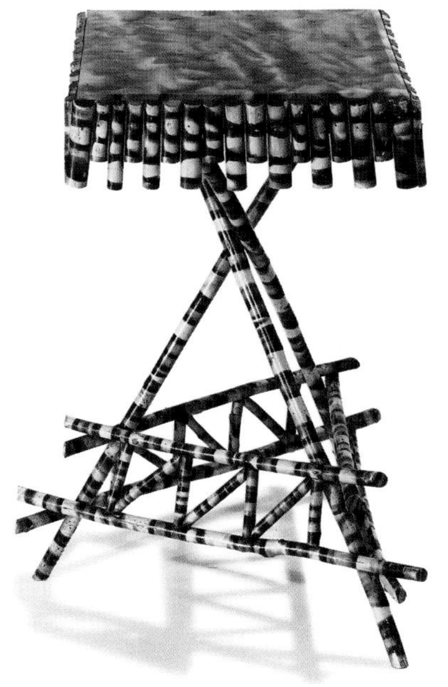

Rustic Table, 1900–20

Anonymous
Painted twigs with black and gray smoked
decoration, branches, and nails
28¾ x 16¾ x 16¾ in.

Brooklyn Museum of Art;
H. Randolph Lever Fund

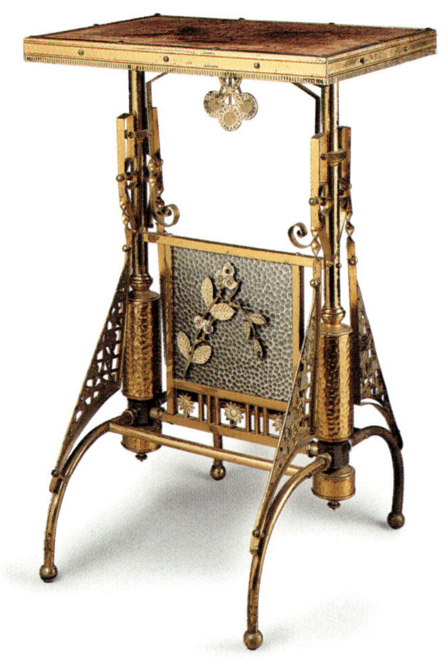

TABLE, 1880
Anonymous, for The Charles Parker Company
Brass, other metals, wood, and fabric
29 x 19 x 17½ in.

Brooklyn Museum of Art;
H. Randolph Lever Fund

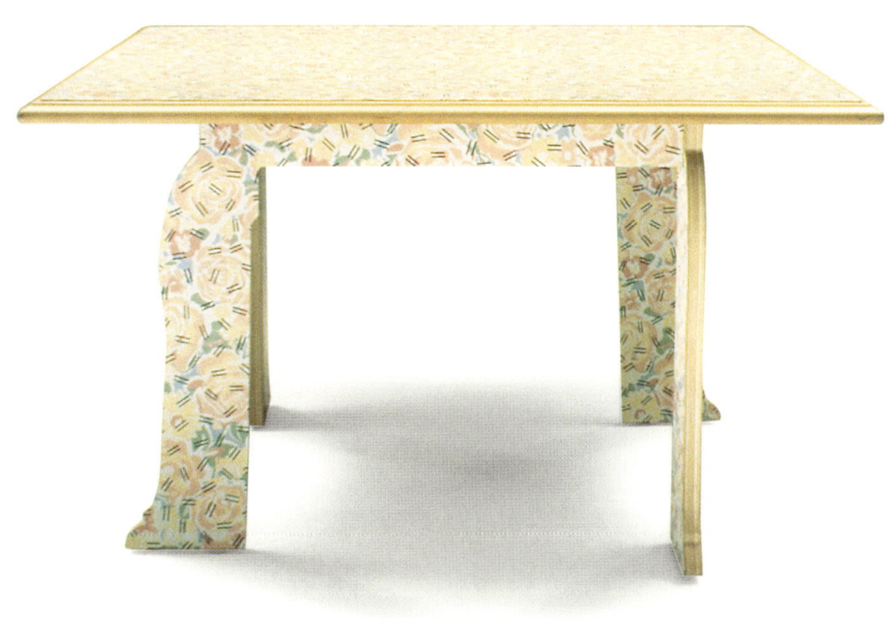

CABRIOLE LEG TABLE, 1984
Robert Venturi, for Knoll, Inc.
Laminated wood, veneer
Grandmother floral pattern
28½ x 48 x 48 in.
Price in 1988: $2200

Knoll Inc.

EXHIBITED TABLE
Laminated wood, veneer
Bird's-eye maple, stained dark gray

Knoll Museum

Though separated by more than a century, Frame Table 68 by Donald Judd (from 1989) and an anonymous Shaker table (from 1850-60) are both simple and spare in design. The Shakers eschewed unnecessary ornamental flourishes as emblems of human pride in the face of the divine. Judd's table reflects the minimalist aesthetics of his own art and era in its form, finish, and apparently seamless joinery techniques.

Another simple, anonymous table (c. 1880) is comparable externally with these two, but again the history and intentions differ. This unique table was made for a family from a tree felled on its estate: "In the place where the tree falleth, there it shall be…" reads an inscription in Liberty style lettering that runs along the fascia. The inspiration for its lack of ornamentation comes from the English Arts and Crafts movement, which also influenced later American Arts and Crafts designs from the Stickley and Roycroft firms.

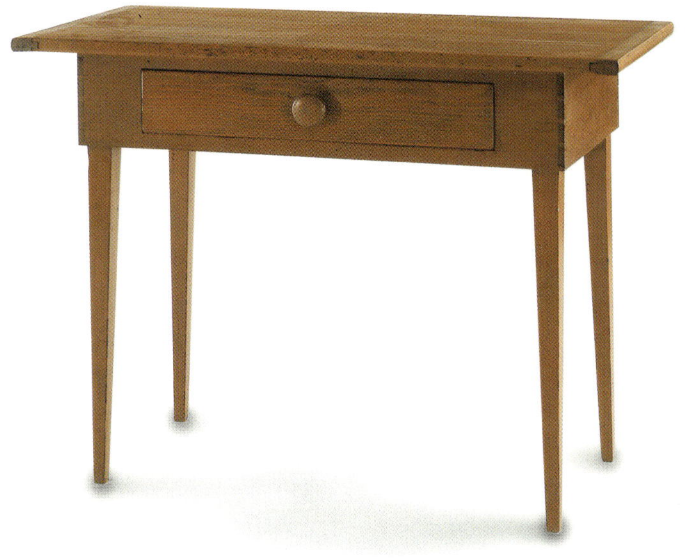

TABLE, 1850–60
Anonymous Shaker
Pine
28⅛ x 39¼ x 18½ in.

**From the Collections of Henry Ford
Museum & Greenfield Village**

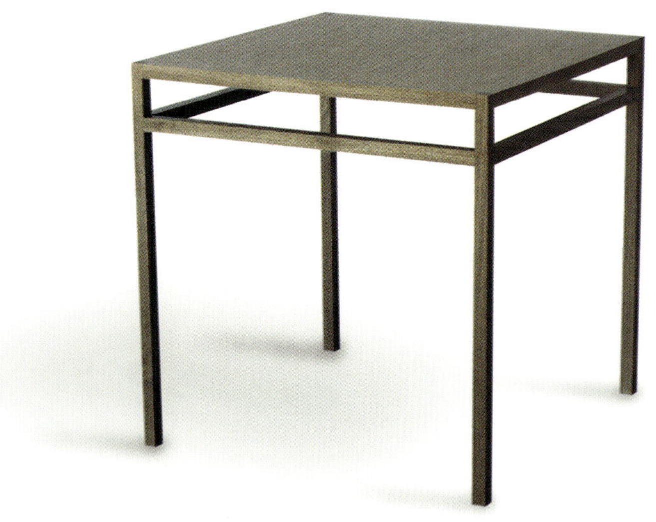

FRAME TABLE 68, 1989
Donald Judd
Oak
29½ x 29½ x 29½ in.
Price in 1989: $2250

Collection of the Donald Judd Estate
©The Donald Judd Estate 1998 /
Licensed by Vaga, NYC

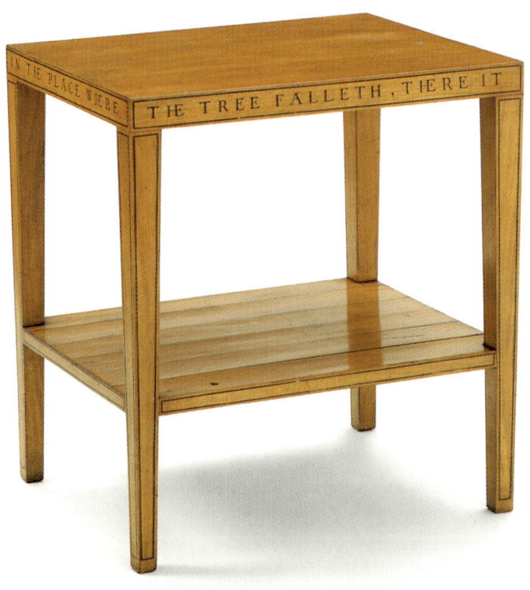

Table, c. 1880
Anonymous
Oak; inscription: "IN THE PLACE WHERE
THE TREE FALLETH, THERE IT SHALL BE
WOODENETHE CLADRASTIS TINCTO RIA…"
27¾ x 27 x 20 in.

Museum of Fine Arts, Boston;
Gift of Aimeé and Rosamond Lamb

Along with their primary role as supporting surfaces, many tables also provide storage with drawers or shelves in various arrangements, as can be seen throughout the exhibition. Several early modern designers experimented with separating storage, surface, and structure. In the 1934 desk by Gilbert Rohde, the metal frame is clearly called out as a structure that supports the black laminate top. The abstract floating volume for storage is suspended from the top and anchored to the legs of one side. The structure recalls Marcel Breuer's groundbreaking explorations with tubular steel in Europe, as well as the work of Kem Weber. From the same year, Weber's dramatic vanity table in streamline chrome and painted wood also separates frame from storage. The large circular mirror is similarly set apart, held aloft by three asymmetrically placed bars of flat steel.

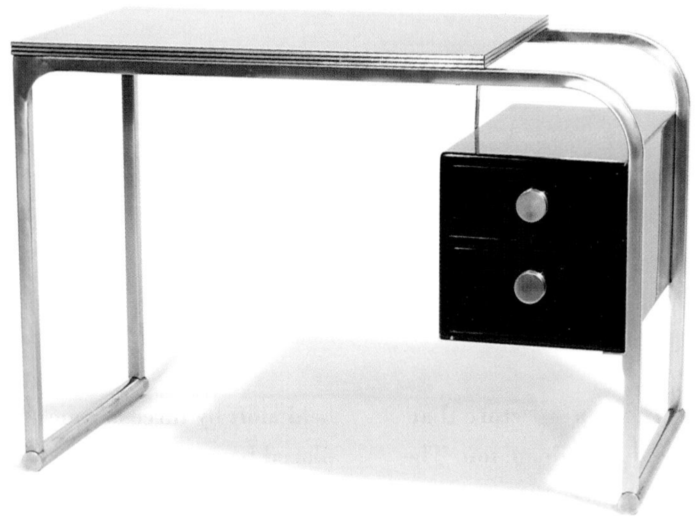

DESK, c. 1934
Gilbert Rohde, for Troy Sunshade
Company, Troy, OH
Polished and chromed steel, wood,
and black plastic laminate
29 x 42 x 22 in.

Brooklyn Museum of Art;
The Brooklyn Museum Fund

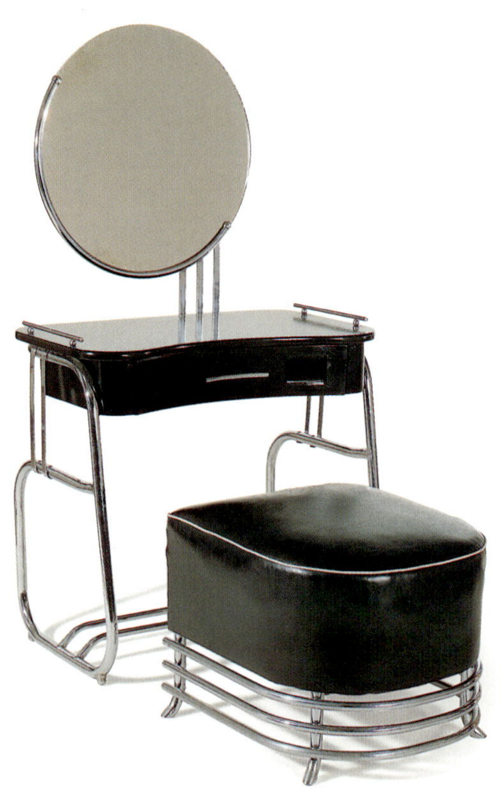

VANITY TABLE 1934
Kem Weber, for Lloyd Manufacturing Company,
Manominee, MI
Tubular and chrome-plated steel,
painted wood, and mirror
55 x 33 x 19½ in.

Brooklyn Museum of Art;
Modernism Benefit Fund

In later experiments with storage, Charles and Ray Eames developed modular forms for use in a component approach also seen in the design of their own house. Made of brightly colored laminates, the storage units appear interchangeable and independent from the support in a modular desk from 1954. Manufactured and marketed by the Herman Miller Furniture Company, the desk became an icon of mid-century modern design. Its forms and colors are recalled in Daven Joy's side table 114 from 1996. The materials have changed to include neoprene veneers and stainless steel, but the antecedents for Joy's modular, planar design are clear.

The lamp table with planter by George Nelson, also for Herman Miller, combines storage and lighting with cabinetry that is emblematic of the late forties and early fifties. A current interpretation of this multifunction formula is seen in David Khouri's *Sexy Sadie* table, which serves as a nightlight and phone table. Leaving on the light eliminates fumbling for a ringing phone in the dark.

The modest little *Hatten* end table offers container and support in a contemporary mass-produced and mass-marketed table. It has a translucent, fluted, hatbox-like volume supported on tubular metal legs and a removable top that can be used as a serving tray. The table follows in the tradition of transformable, multipurpose furniture and shows the continuing use of plastic as an inexpensive, malleable material in American design.

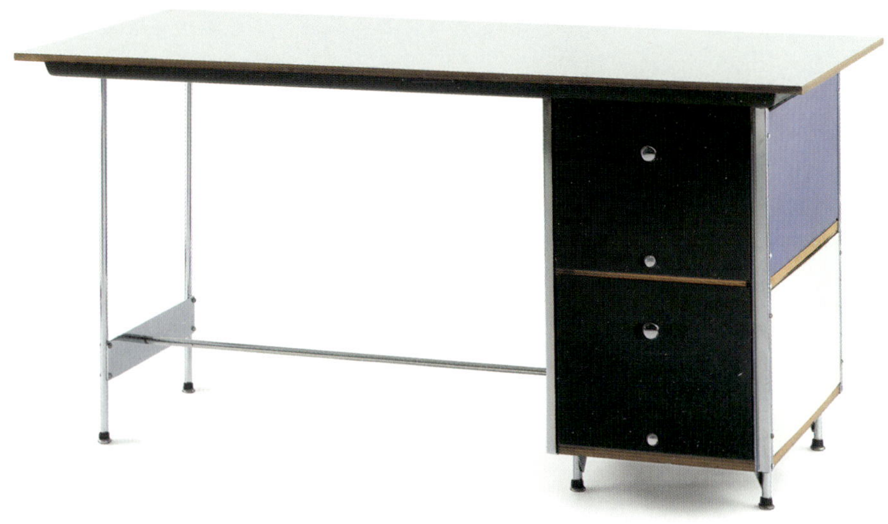

**MODULAR DESK,
EAMES STORAGE UNITS, c. 1954**
Charles and Ray Eames, for Herman
Miller Furniture Company
Wood, laminate, micarta,
and chrome-plated metal
60 x 28 x 29¾ in.

From the Collections of Henry Ford
Museum & Greenfield Village

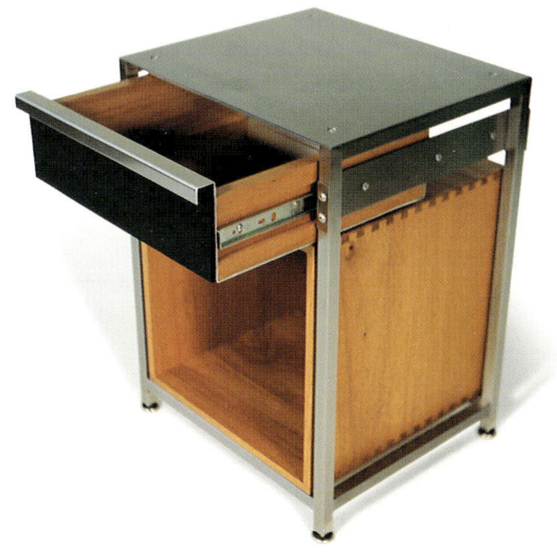

SIDE TABLE 114, 1996
Daven Joy and Trav Ebling, for Park Furniture
Maple, stainless steel, and red neoprene
21 x 16 x 14 in.
Price in 1998: $2265

Courtesy of Daven Joy and Park Furniture

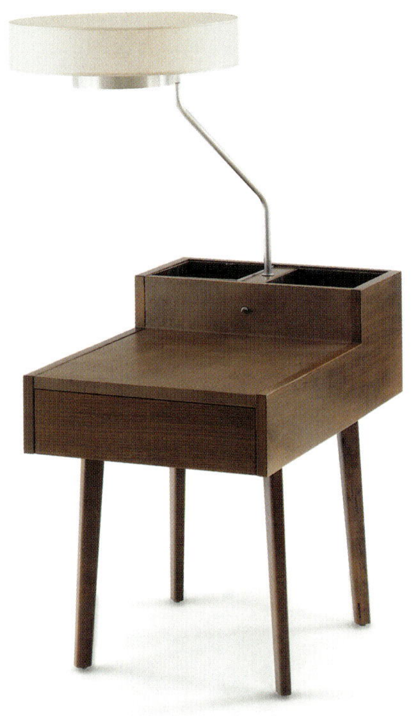

LAMP TABLE, 1947–55
George Nelson, for Herman Miller
Furniture Company
Wood, leather, and fluorescent lamp
47 x19 x 30 in.
Price in 1947: $55

From the Collections of Henry Ford
Museum & Greenfield Village

RIGHT

SEXY SADIE NIGHT TABLE, 1998
David Khouri, for Comma
MDF, lacquer, acrylic, and fluorescent lamp
27 x 14 x 17 in.
Price in 1998: $2150

Courtesy of Comma

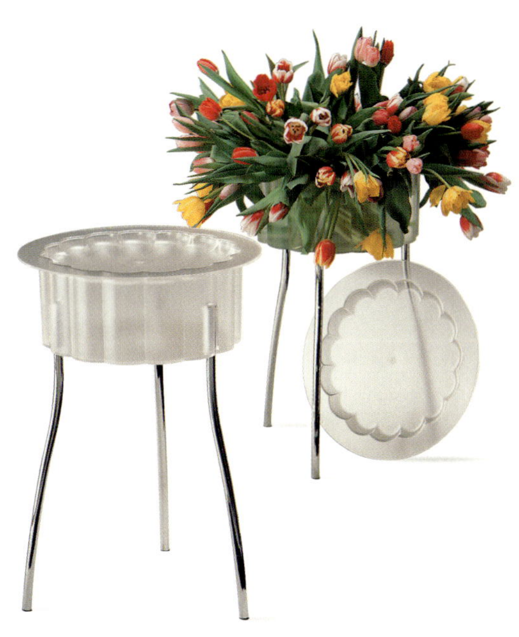

HATTEN END TABLE, 1993
Ehlén Johansson, for IKEA
Acrylic, tubular metal
23 x 15¾ in.
Price in 1998: $39.95

oth of these early-nineteenth-century tables could have been found in the living room or parlor of a well-to-do Boston family, and both have forms adapted to specific functions. The lady's work table incorporates storage space in a fabric bag that hangs below the table's hard top. The soft-sided bag could contain the irregularly shaped materials—needles, fabric, balls of yarn, hoops—involved in sewing or needlework. The tops of such "bag" tables often were decorated with painted landscape scenes. Like vanities, these tables were used only by woman; writing tables and secretaries in contrast were made for men and women in different sizes. The convertible game and work table could function as a work surface (with leaves that extend to hold candles for lighting), an adjustable felt-covered writing table, or a game table with inlaid boards for backgammon and chess. This table also has storage space, which might have been used for sewing or writing materials, but in a hard case. Either table would have been a sign of status, showing that the owners had sufficient leisure and means to play games, entertain, or indulge interests in needlework and crewelwork.

Although specifically designed as a game board, Isamu Noguchi's 1947 chess table for the Herman Miller Furniture Company also could be used for multiple purposes—and suggests no preference among the sexes. An early publicity photo, however, shows a woman seated before the table, with the hidden storage drawer open to reveal needles and thread strewn among the checker dots. The table recalls Noguchi's interlocking, curvilinear sculptures of the same period and similarly relates to the surrealist fascination with undulating, organic forms. Such forms are prefigured in architect Frederick Kiesler's nesting coffee table from 1938. With its interpenetrating kidney shapes and cast aluminum construction, the two-unit table is experimental in form and material, not unlike Kiesler's later organic "Endless House" project.

The granite cooktop by Bruce Tomb takes the tradition of tables for very specific use and storage functions in an inventive direction. A salvaged fire extinguisher below the table's surface holds the propane that fuels the burners. The historical and industrial associations suggest a recasting of the lady's work table for a *Blade Runner* domesticity.

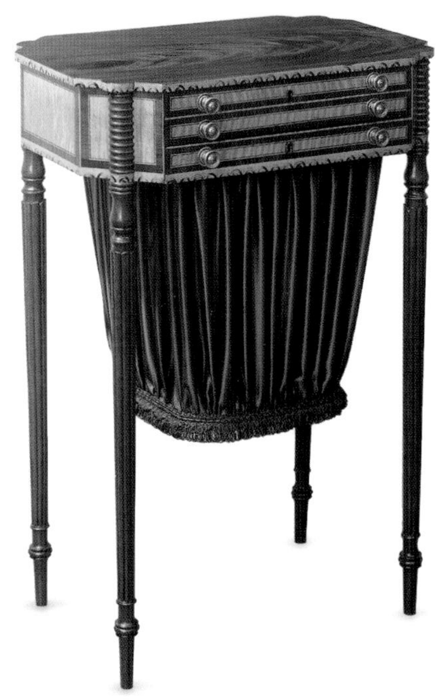

Lady's Work Table, c. 1800
Anonymous
African mahogany, satinwood,
silk, and brass fittings
29 x 15¾ x 20 in.

Museum of Fine Arts, Boston;
The M. and M. Karolik Collection
of 18th Century American Arts

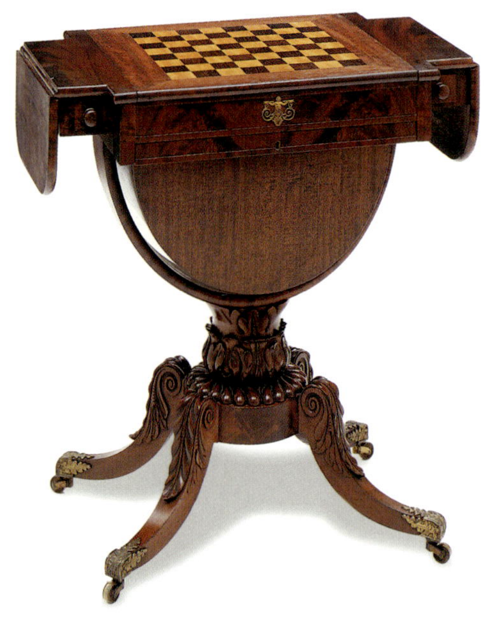

GAME AND WORK TABLE, c. 1820–30
Anonymous
Mahogany with inlay, brass fittings
30 x 40¼ x 17 in.

Museum of Fine Arts, Boston;
Gift of William N. Banks and Frank Bemis Fund

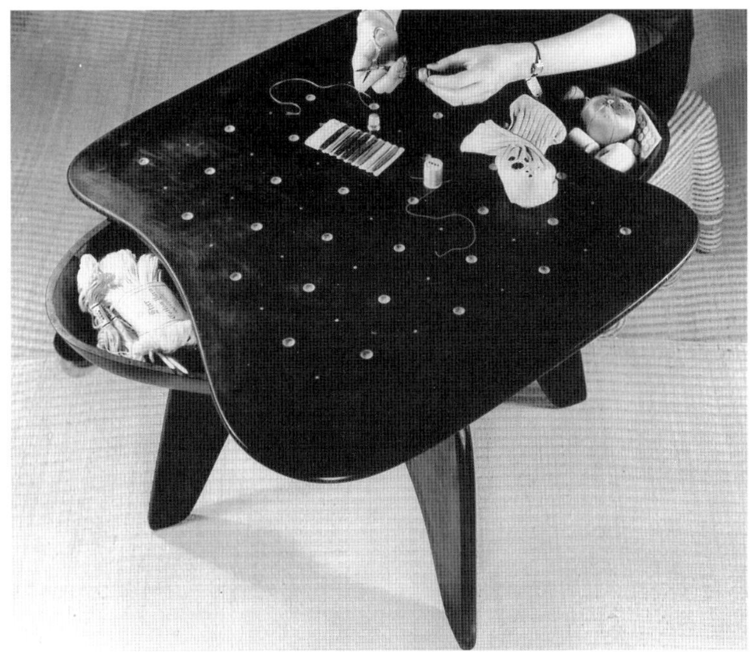

CHESS TABLE, MODEL NO. IN 61, 1947
Isamu Noguchi, for Herman Miller
Furniture Company
Ebonized plywood, aluminum, and plastic
19¼ x 33⅞ x 30⁹⁄₁₆ in.
Price in 1948: $158

Photo courtesy of The Isamu Noguchi
Foundation, Inc.

EXHIBITED TABLE
Musée des Arts Décoratifs de Montréal;
Gift of Jay Spectre, by exchange

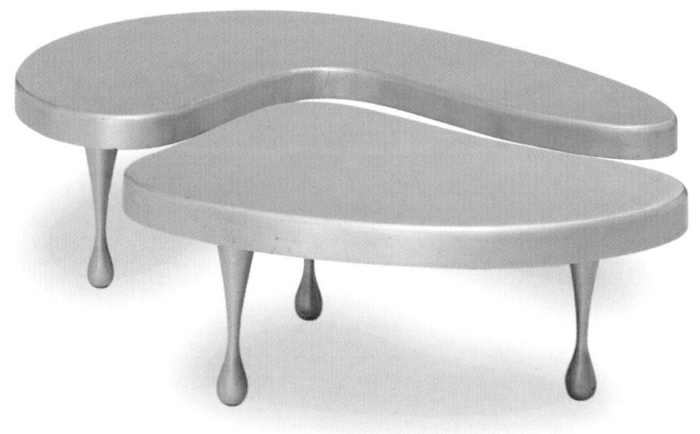

NESTING **C**OFFEE **T**ABLE, 1938
Frederick Kiesler
Cast aluminum
9½ x 34 x 25 in.; 9½ x 22 x 16¼ in.

The Museum of Modern Art, New York;
Gift of Carlo M. Grossman and
Josie G. Lindau in memory of their
parents, Isobel and Isidore Grossman

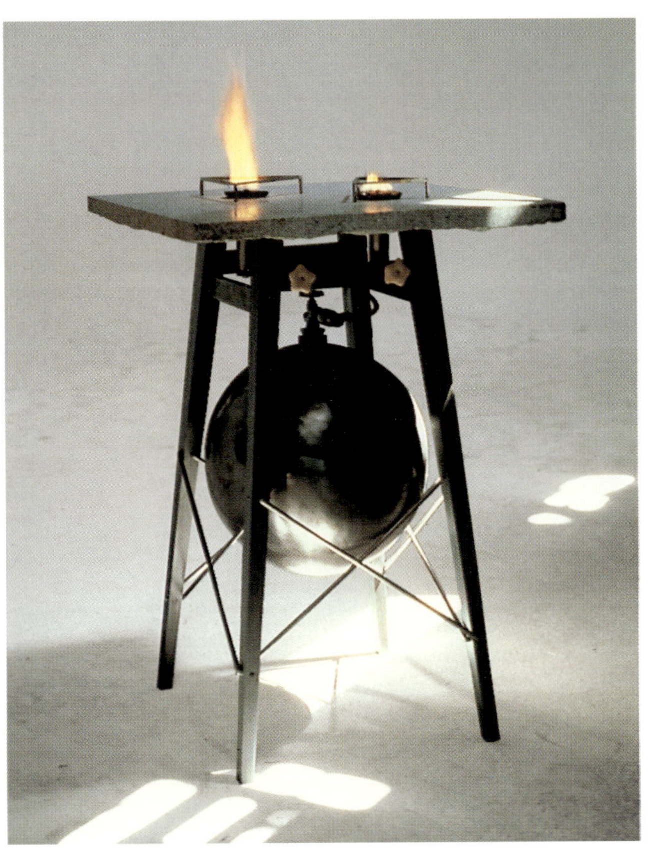

Granite Cooktop, 1985

Bruce Tomb
Granite, maple, stainless steel, plastic, and
components: camp stove parts, tank from
salvaged fire extinguisher vessel from
Lockheed Co. Bomber, propane gas
40 x 29 x 29 in.

Collection of Interim Office of Architecture,
John Randolph and Bruce Tomb

With its curvilinear vegetal
forms and flared tree
trunk base, the anony-
mous mahogany game
table from the turn of the century is a
rare example of American art nouveau
design. It makes an improbable pair
with a classic of high modern furnish-
ing—Eero Saarinen's 1956 dining
table for Knoll. Yet in both cases
the tables seem to grow from their
pedestal bases. Saarinen thought that
"the underside of typical chairs and
tables makes a confusing, unrestful
world," and his pedestal series was his
effort "to clear up the slum of legs."[2]
Richard Schultz, also designing for
Knoll, put a pop art spin on the forms
of base, trunk, and top in his *Petal
Table*. He gave the forms Saarinen
had abstracted a more recognizable,
organic slant, recalling the naturalistic
carving of the earlier table.

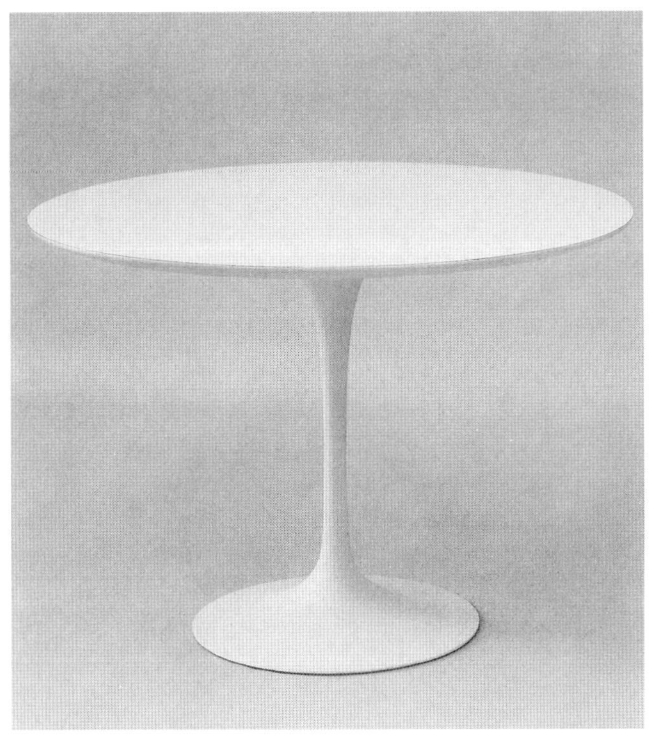

Dining Table, 1956
Eero Saarinen, for Knoll, Inc.
Coated cast aluminum, marble

Exhibited Table
White cast aluminum, white laminate
42¼ x 28¼ in.
Price in 1998: $1627 (new table)

Courtesy of Knoll, Inc.

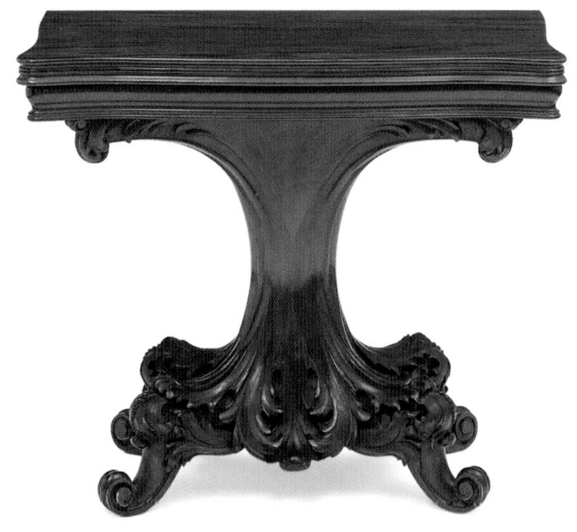

CARD TABLE, 1890–1900
Anonymous, for Tobey Furniture Company
Mahogany
29¾ x 36 x 18¼ in.

Museum of Fine Arts, Boston;
Anonymous Gift and Helen
and Alice Colburn Fund

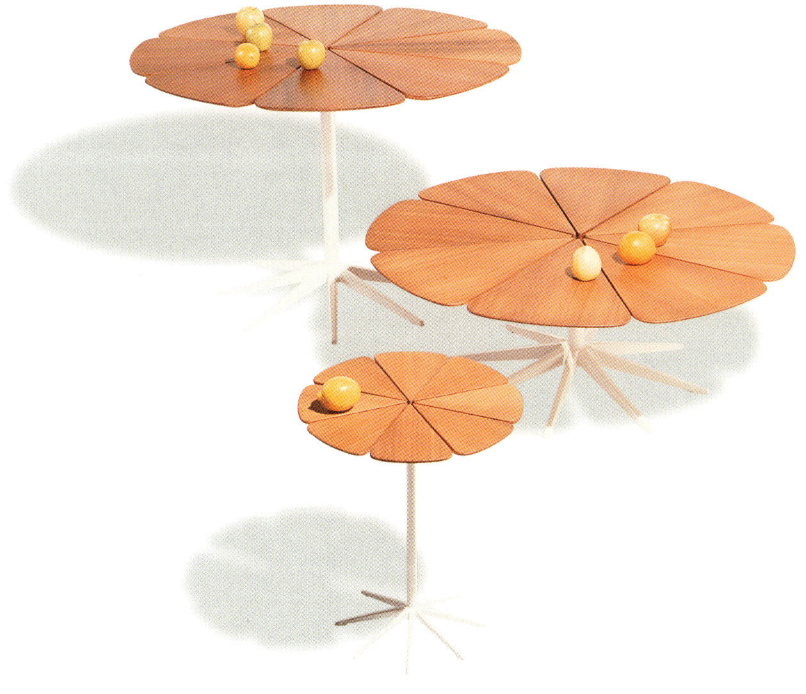

PETAL TABLE, 1960
Richard Schultz, for Knoll, Inc.
Metal base, white fused plastic finish,
and redwood top
19 x 16 in.
Price in 1974: $104

Courtesy of Richard Schultz

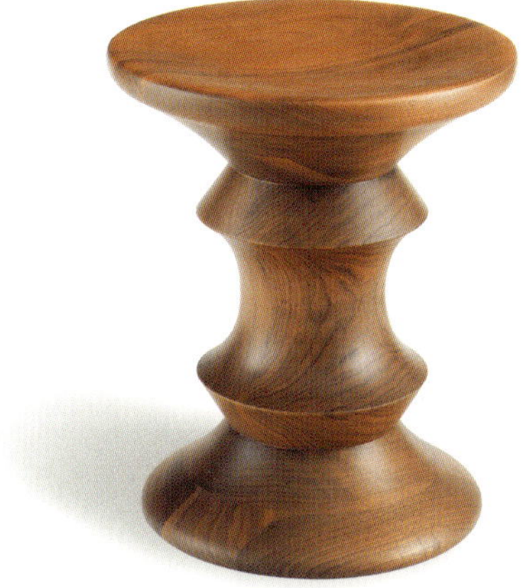

tones from Maya Lin's *The Earth is (not) Flat* collection shows this artist's continuing interest in interconnections between the natural environment and human activities. She derived the shape and materiality of the slightly concave, cast concrete form from the pre-Columbian *metate*, an ancient stone chair.[3] The Eameses' stool from 1960, which like Lin's can double as a table, also suggests primal, non-European sources in its forms. The use of solid wood recalls totemic sculpture and gives full expression to this traditional furniture material. Left in a natural state, the wood offered a counterpoint to the angular glass and steel of the corporate interior where the stool was first used, the lobby of the Time-Life Building in New York.

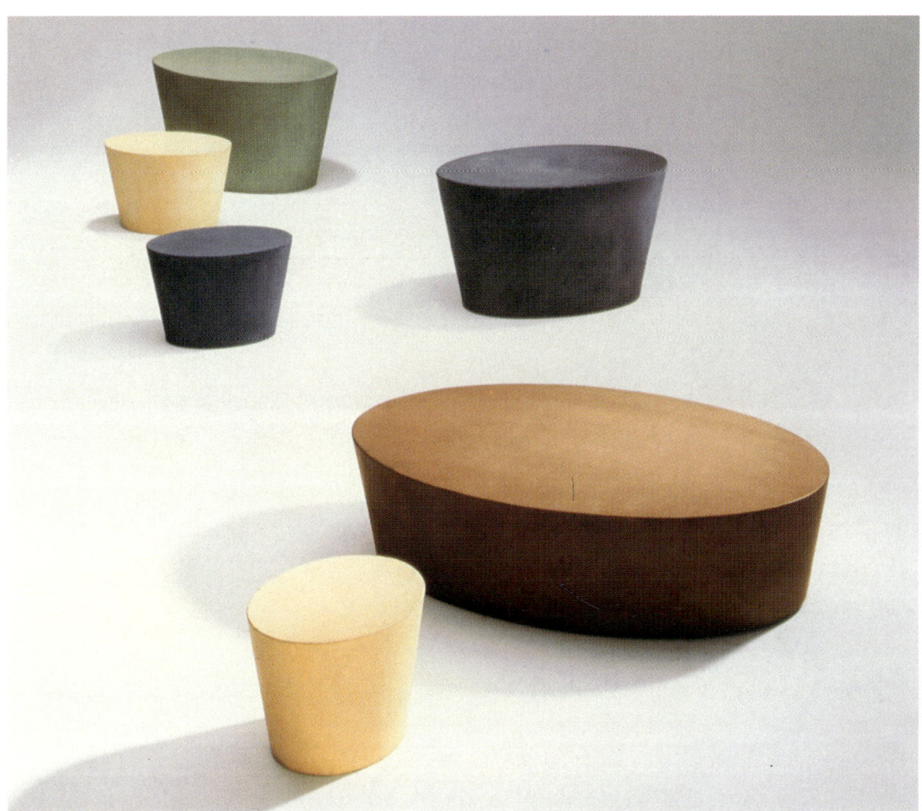

Stool, from Occasional Tables, 1960

Charles and Ray Eames,
for Herman Miller Furniture Company
Solid walnut
15 x 13 in.
Price in 1961: $108

From the Collections of Henry Ford Museum
& Greenfield Village

Stones, 1998

Maya Lin, for Knoll, Inc.
Spray-molded fiberglass-reinforced cement with
integral color, polystyrene filler material, integral
UV stabilized pigmented color, and UV-retardant
water sealer top coating

EXHIBITED TABLE
Adult Seat, from *Stones*, 1998
15 x 27 x 19 in.
Price in 1998: $795

Courtesy of Knoll, Inc.

Karim Rashid uses colored glass in three different geometric shapes to transform the traditional nesting table in his *Tri-Spectra* design from 1997. He exploits the notion of stacking and the transparency of the material to produce different colors of refracted light. According to the wishes of the owner, the glass tables can be re-positioned, changing the overall configuration of the ensemble. Rashid employs a laminated glass technique, with colored film fused between layers of glass. M. Ali Tayar also investigates material and production possibilities in his prototype *NEA Table 2* from 1994. The material is an equivalent of particleboard made from recycled wood shavings. "To create the quintessential ready-made object and also develop a system of affordable furniture, he chose a stock particleboard pallet of the type used in the food industry for transporting goods to market."[4] The shape of the table is open to the plastic possibilities of molding but also "dictated by function." Fitted with legs and topped with a clear glass sheet, it becomes a dining table.

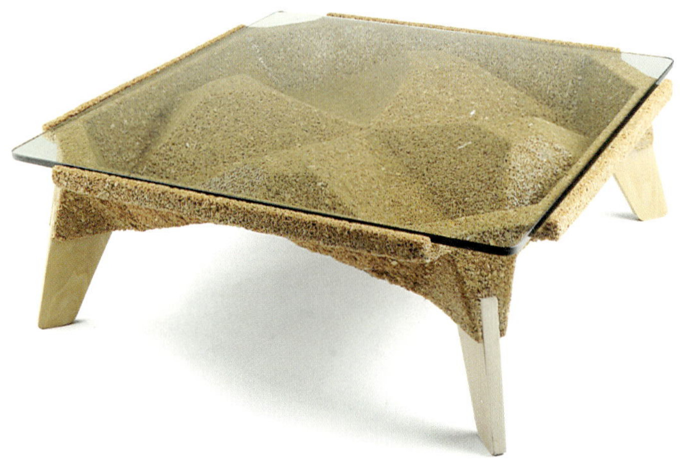

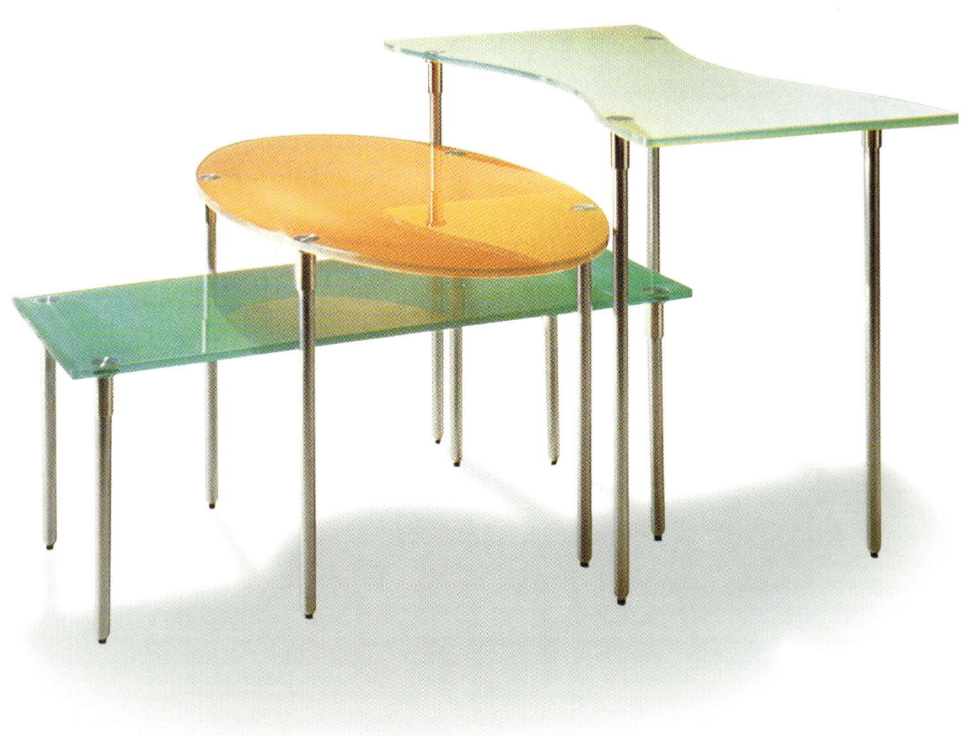

Tri-Spectra, 1998
Karim Rashid, for Zeritalia®
Aluminum, glass sheets colored with
water-based paints, and Colorglass™ System
23⅕ x 34 x 34 in.
Price in 1998: $1499

Courtesy of Curvet USA, Inc.

LEFT

NEA Table 2, 1994
M. Ali Tayar
Molded particleboard base,
hardwood legs, and glass tabletop
15 x 30 x 30 in.

Courtesy of Parallel Design Partnership;
made possible by a National Endowment
for the Arts grant

The Tea Leaf pattern ironstone was made in England from 1856 until the turn of the century solely for export to the United States and Canada. "The copper luster decorative motifs were applied to add variety and interest" to a range of familiar, standard shapes.[5] This selection shows the elaborate services commonly used in the mid-nineteenth century. Although this kind of sturdy ironstone was intended for lower- or middle-class households, the variety of cups, plates, platters, and bowls demonstrates careful attention to formal rituals of dining in imitation of the upper classes. The number and specificity of the pieces—including posset cups (for a drink of hot milk curdled with wine or ale), relish trays, several tureens, compotes, waste bowls, and bone receptacle—attest to an elaboration similar to that of services in finer porcelain. Elaborate dining services remained standard through the century, with the number of pieces determined by whether food was served by servants or the family: service *à la Française* or *à la Russe*.

In the late twentieth century elaborate porcelain dinnerware continues to be used in certain formal situations. A renowned set was the Reagan presidential china produced by Lenox in 1981 to serve 220 with 19-piece place settings and a total of 4,372 pieces. (There are relatively few serving pieces compared with the earlier ironstone set, since guests would be served rather than serving themselves.) This official state service is decorated in twenty-four carat gold with a lattice diaper pattern on the rim of each service plate and the presidential seal on the pieces of each place setting. The china was designed by Lenox in consultation with Nancy Reagan, and the shade of scarlet is distinctively hers.[6] Joan Didion asserts that "one of the reasons Mrs. Reagan [says she] ordered the famous new china was because…the Johnson China had no finger bowls."[7] Also without finger bowls is the simple and nearly indestructible set of *Lifetime* ware (1947). Made of melamine, a durable thermosetting plastic, dishes such as these found their way into many homes in the postwar era, taking their place alongside colorful spun aluminum tumblers, Tupperware, and TV trays.

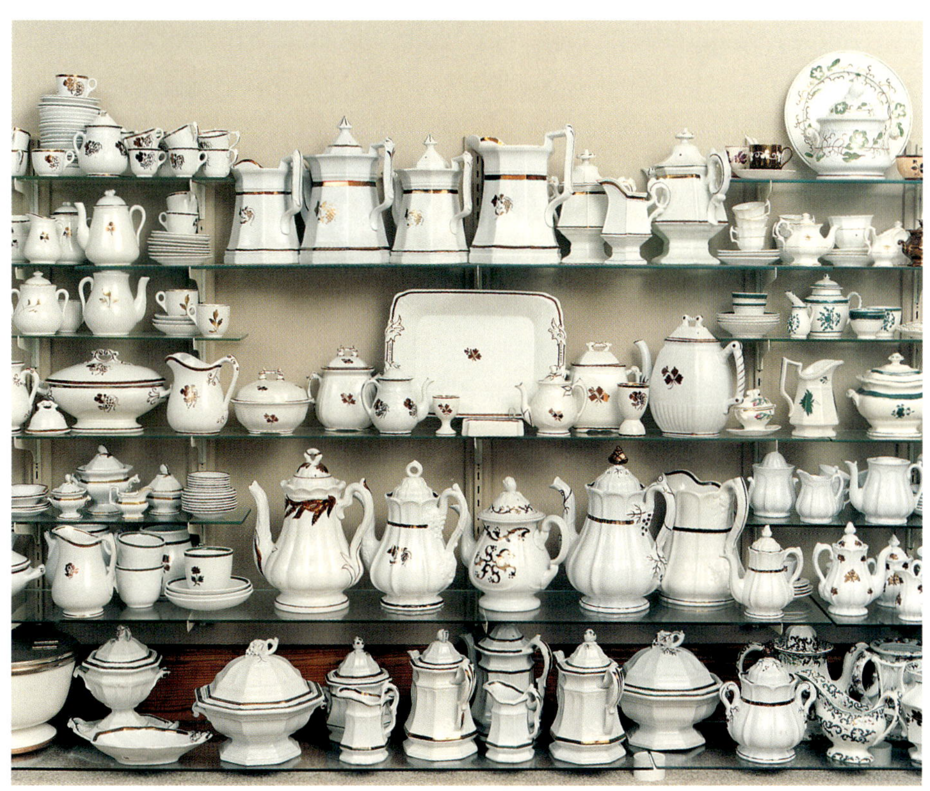

Tea Leaf Ironstone China, and Variants, 1856–1900

Numerous potters
White ironstone with copper luster decoration

Collection of Dale Abrams

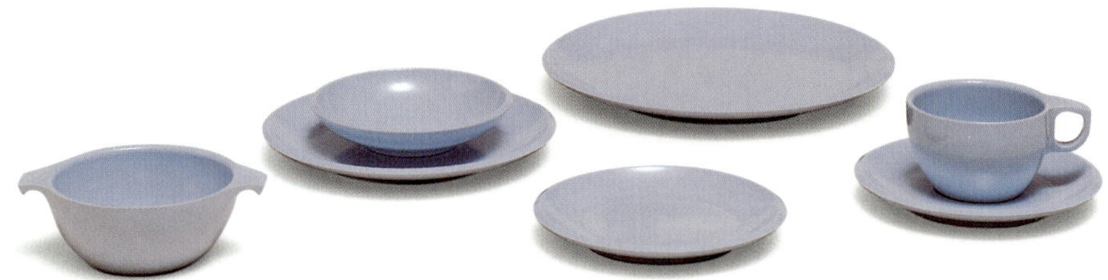

LIFETIME WARE, 1947
Jon Hedu, for The Watertown
Manufacturing Company
Melamine

The Museum of Modern Art, New York;
Gift of George E. Weigl Co.

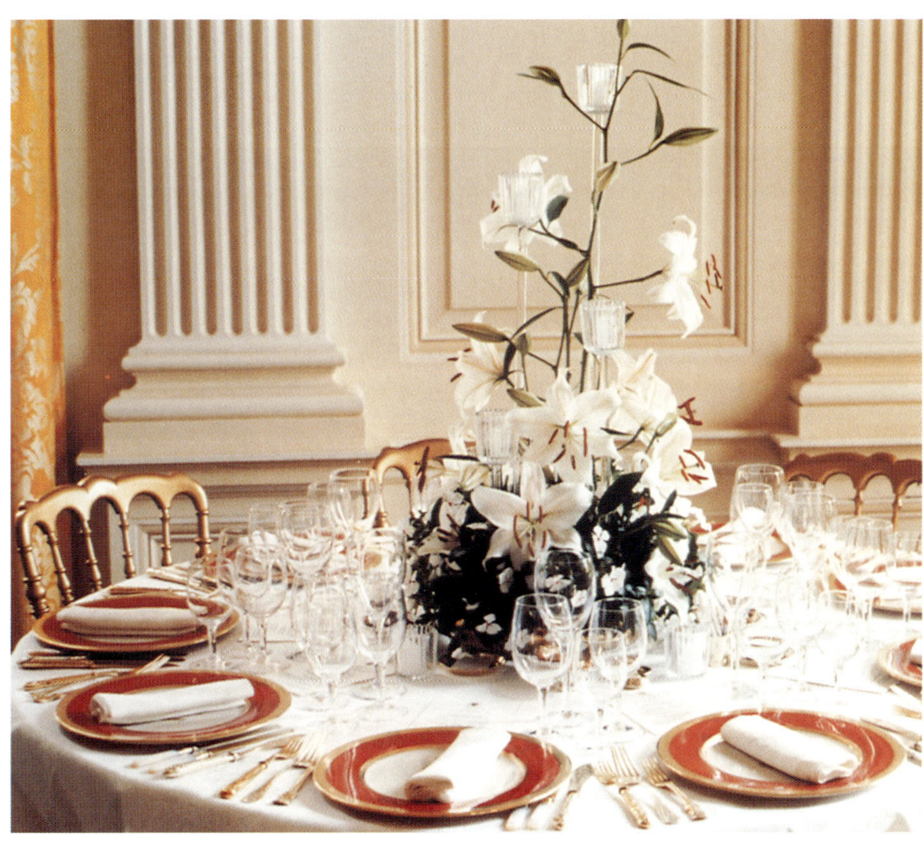

REAGAN SERVICE FOR
THE WHITE HOUSE, 1981
Lenox China
Fine china with scarlet red and 24 karat
gold banding

EXHIBITED TABLEWARE
Lenox China Archives, Lenox Brands

The four art pottery vases in the exhibition reveal the access average American consumers had to a variety of styles in mass-produced pieces that retained associations with artisan-made crafts. The vase produced by the Rookwood Pottery uses the stylized floral and architectural motifs popular in Arts and Crafts design. The piece from the Pewabic Pottery is distinguished by the free-flowing, abstract treatment of the luster glaze. Glazing is also the most unusual aspect of the vase by Charles Clewell, a potter who used shape blanks available from other ceramic companies. Clewell experimented with a copper-plated finish that produced a metallic sheen, later with a green patina. The vase manufactured by Muncie Pottery is a radical design for popular consumption. Appearing like *Nude Descending a Staircase* in ceramic, it is unusual for introducing European high art antecedents into the popular market.

The differences between the vases mark a major division in ceramic design: the distinction between shape and surface. The Muncie and Rookwood vases emphasize shape; the Clewell and Pewabic, surface and color. Color is clearly the point with *Fiesta*, issued first in 1936 and reissued in 1986. Although the shapes have a deco lineage, color (especially the infamously radioactive red glaze) was *Fiesta*'s main feature. The tumblers in the exhibition are simple tubular forms in the extravagant tropical tones of the six original colors. A similar approach to abstract form is evident in the double egg cups from Lu-Ray Pastels, another broadly available consumer line. (The small end holds soft-boiled eggs; the large end, poached.) As the "Pastels" in the name implies, this tableware offered a fashionable alternative for modern tables in softer, less neon, colors.

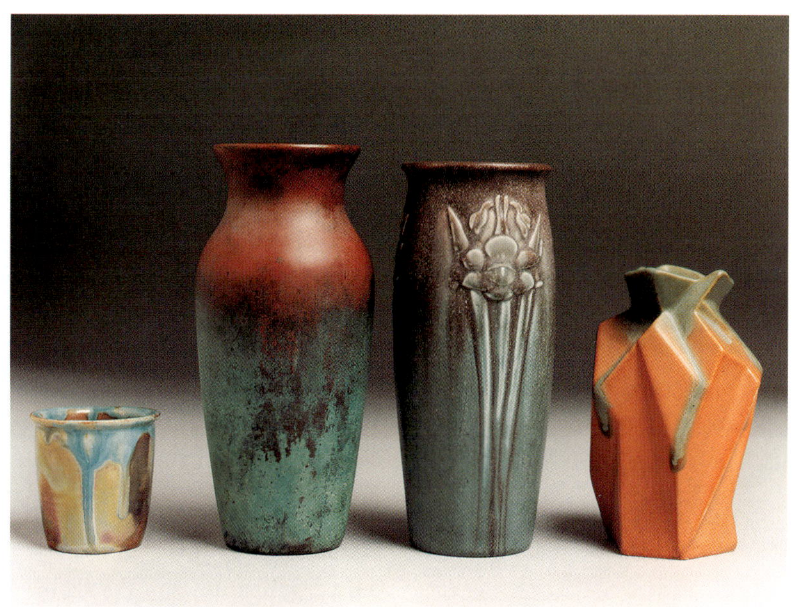

VASE, early 20th century
Anonymous, for Pewabic Pottery, Detroit, MI
Ceramic
3 x 4 x 1½ in.

Collection of Steve M. Shellabarger

VASE, c. 1923
Charles Walter Clewell, for Clewell Metal Art,
Canton, OH
Ceramic
8¾ x 6¼ x 2 in.

Collection of Steve M. Shellabarger

VASE, early 20th century
Anonymous, for Rookwood Pottery
Ceramic
8½ x 5½ x 2½ in.

Collection of Steve M. Shellabarger

VASE, c. 1930
Anonymous, for Muncie Pottery, Muncie, IN
Ceramic
6½ x 6 x 2 in.

Collection of Steve M. Shellabarger

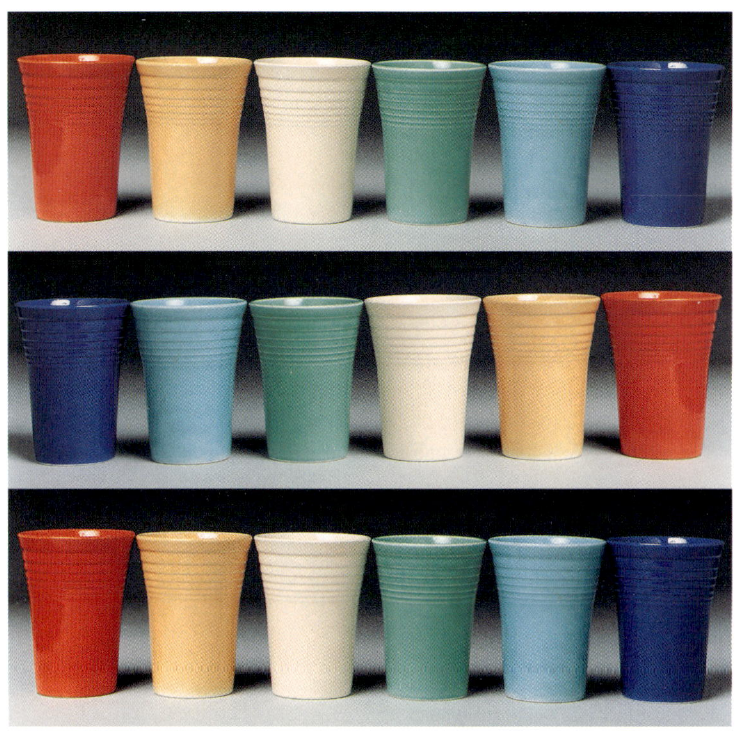

Fiesta Juice Tumblers, 1936
Fredrick Rhead, et al., for Homer
Laughlin China Company, Newell, WV
Ceramic
Set of six

Collection of Steve M. Shellabarger

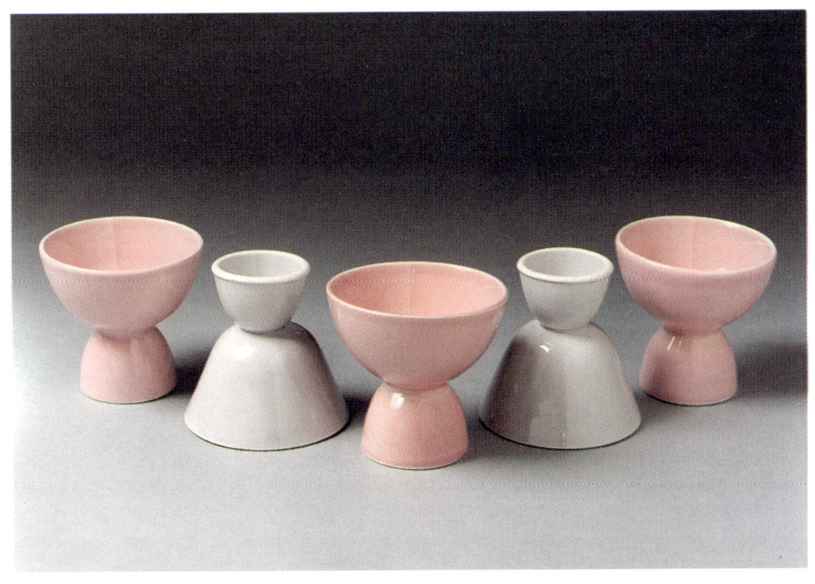

DOUBLE EGG CUPS, 1939
Lu-Ray Pastels, U.S.A., for Taylor Smith & Taylor
Ceramic
Set of five
Price in 1948: $0.65 each

Collection of Elliot T. Fishman

Arthur Eugene Baggs, director of Marblehead Pottery in Marblehead, Massachusetts, from 1908 into the 1920s and later a long-time professor of ceramics at The Ohio State University, was a designer who experimented with both form and surface. His vases, for example, use novel shapes and glazes; the red glaze is derived from crushed taillight glass from automobiles.

Eva Zeisel is perhaps best know for her innovative work with shape and surface—and for having such work commercially produced. Her dinnerware produced by Castelton China for the Museum of Modern Art, New York, in 1946, was hailed as "the first translucent china dinnerware, *modern in shape*, produced in the United States."[8] Her investigations followed in the tradition of the modernist atelier, combining advanced material properties—clear glaze on a clay body so vitreous that light is transmitted through it—with simplified forms untouched by decoration. These dishes were used in formal and everyday settings, as were her later, more organic designs for Hall China. Her prototype baby feeding set emphasizes the rounded, globular forms also used by Russel Wright and other designers of the period. The sensuous, asymmetrical baby feeding cup has a wide mouth and is designed to fit between the thumb and index finger of the user, while the hand can wrap around the curved shape of the cup's body. The irregularly shaped oval dish has a combination spoon and ring handle attached to one side.

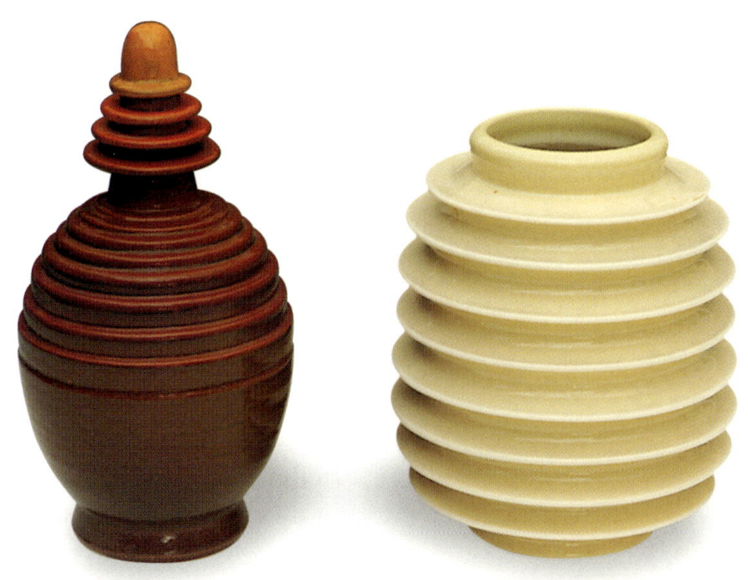

VASE, mid 20th century
Arthur Eugene Baggs, for Marblehead Pottery
Thrown and glazed red earthenware
9¼ x 6¾ in.

The Arthur E. Baggs Memorial Library Collection,
The Ohio State University

VASE, 1942
Arthur Eugene Baggs
Glazed porcelain
8 x 6 in.

The Arthur E. Baggs Memorial Library Collection,
The Ohio State University

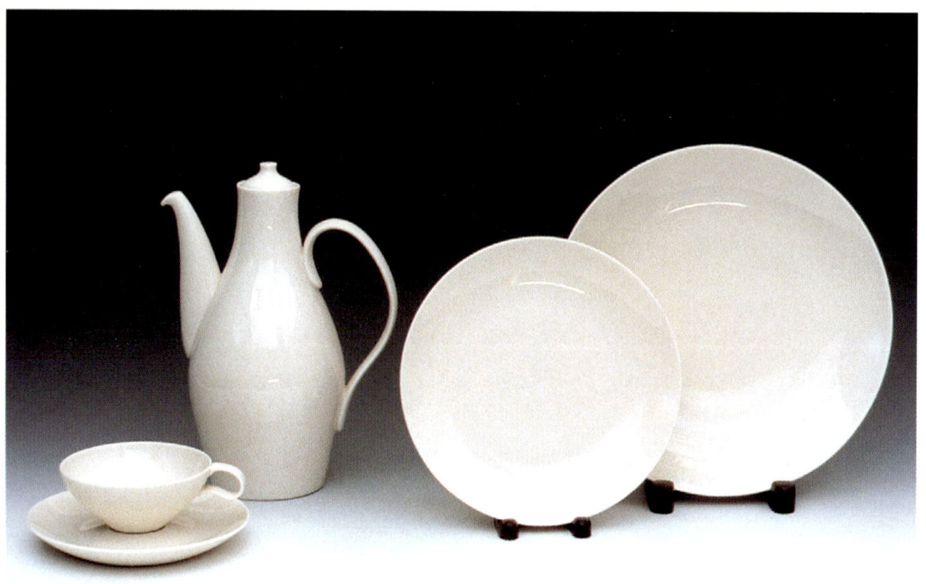

MUSEUM DINNER SERVICE, 1942–1945
Eva Zeisel, for Castleton China Company,
New Castle, PA, for the Museum of Modern Art
Glazed, undecorated porcelain

The Arthur E. Baggs Memorial Library Collection,
The Ohio State University

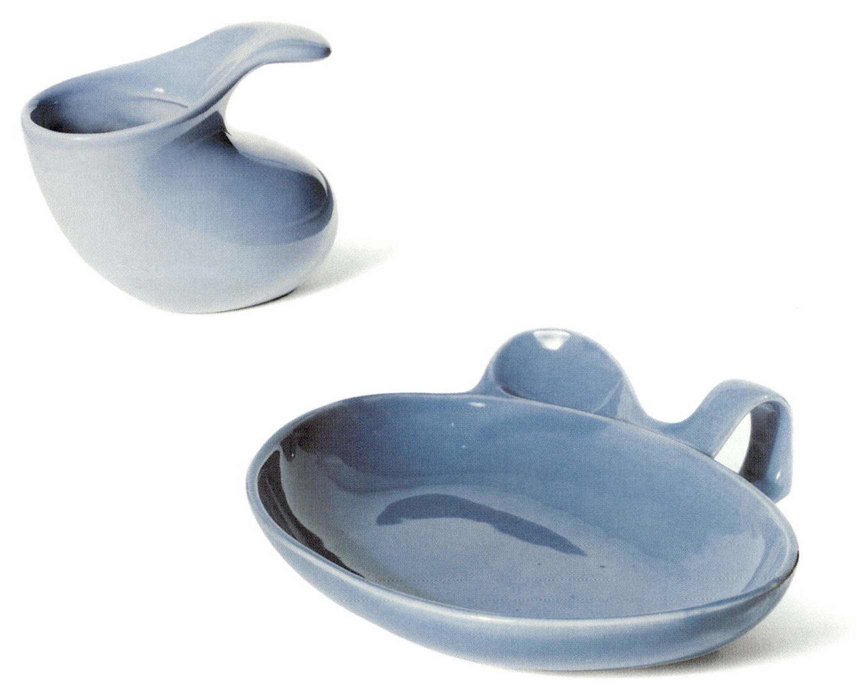

Baby Feeding Cup, c. 1940
Eva Zeisel
Glazed earthenware
3 x 4 x 3 in.

Brooklyn Museum of Art;
Gift of Eva Zeisel

Right
Baby Dish, c. 1940
Eva Zeisel
Glazed earthenware
2 x 8½ x 7¾ in.

Brooklyn Museum of Art;
Gift of Eva Zeisel

1   Descriptive and background information on
    the Marcotte table and the anonymous table
    made of twigs is based on "Purchase
    Recommendations" dated 1986 and 1982
    respectively by Dianne H. Pilgrim in the
    Brooklyn Museum files.

2   Saarinen's comments are quoted in Knoll
    promotional materials on this table.

3   Promotional materials from Knoll mention
    Lin's use of the *metate* form as a source for
    her design.

4   Quotations and descriptive information on
    this table are from Paola Antonelli, *Mutant
    Materials in Contemporary Design* (New
    York: The Museum of Modern Art, 1995),
    p. 101.

5   Dale Abrams, "Tea Leaf Ironstone China,"
    in Dawn Stoltzfus and Jeffrey B. Snyder,
    *White Ironstone: A Survey of its Many
    Forms* (Atglen, PA: Schiffer Publishing
    LTd., 1997), p. 13.

6   Margaret Brown Klapthor, *Official White
    House China 1918 to the Present* (brochure
    for Lenox, Inc., 1994), p. 23. Marcel
    Juillerat is credited as the chief surface
    designer for the line.

7   Joan Didion, *After Henry* (New York:
    Vintage Books, 1993), p. 33.

8   *Everyday Arts Quarterly: A Guide to Well
    Designed Products* no. 2 (Walker Arts
    Center, Minneapolis; fall 1946), p. 5.
    Emphasis in original.

A FOLIO OF TABLES

In the following pages, an invited selection of artists in varied fields (photography, film, music, architecture, literature, art) offer meditations on tables and the memories, rituals, and uses they suggest.

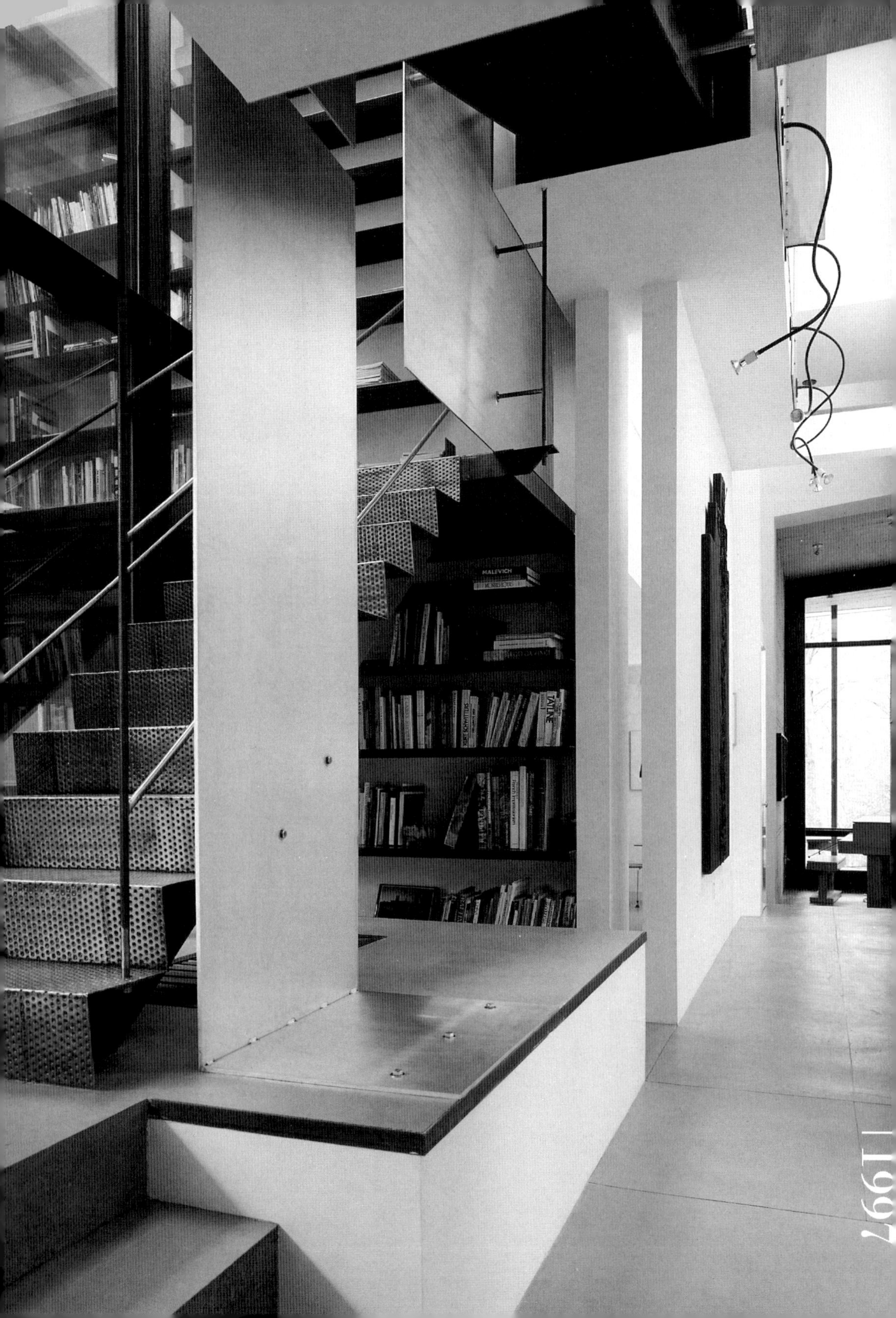

Projects by

TINA BARNEY

GREGG BORDOWITZ

DILLER + SCOFIDIO

ANN HAMILTON

MARTIN SCORSESE

ALLAN WEXLER

VITO ACCONCI

MACK SCOGIN AND MERRILL ELAM

JEFFREY KIPNIS

DAVID LANG

HOLLY BRUBACH

LYNNE COHEN

RANDALL KENAN

GUILLERMO KUITCA

RENNY RAMAKERS

A HOUSE IN MAINE, 1997
Scogin Elam and Bray Architects, Inc.

Courtesy of Scogin Elam and Bray Architects, Inc.

TINA BARNEY

JILL'S BREAKFAST TABLE, 1998

Courtesy of the artist and Janet Borden Inc.

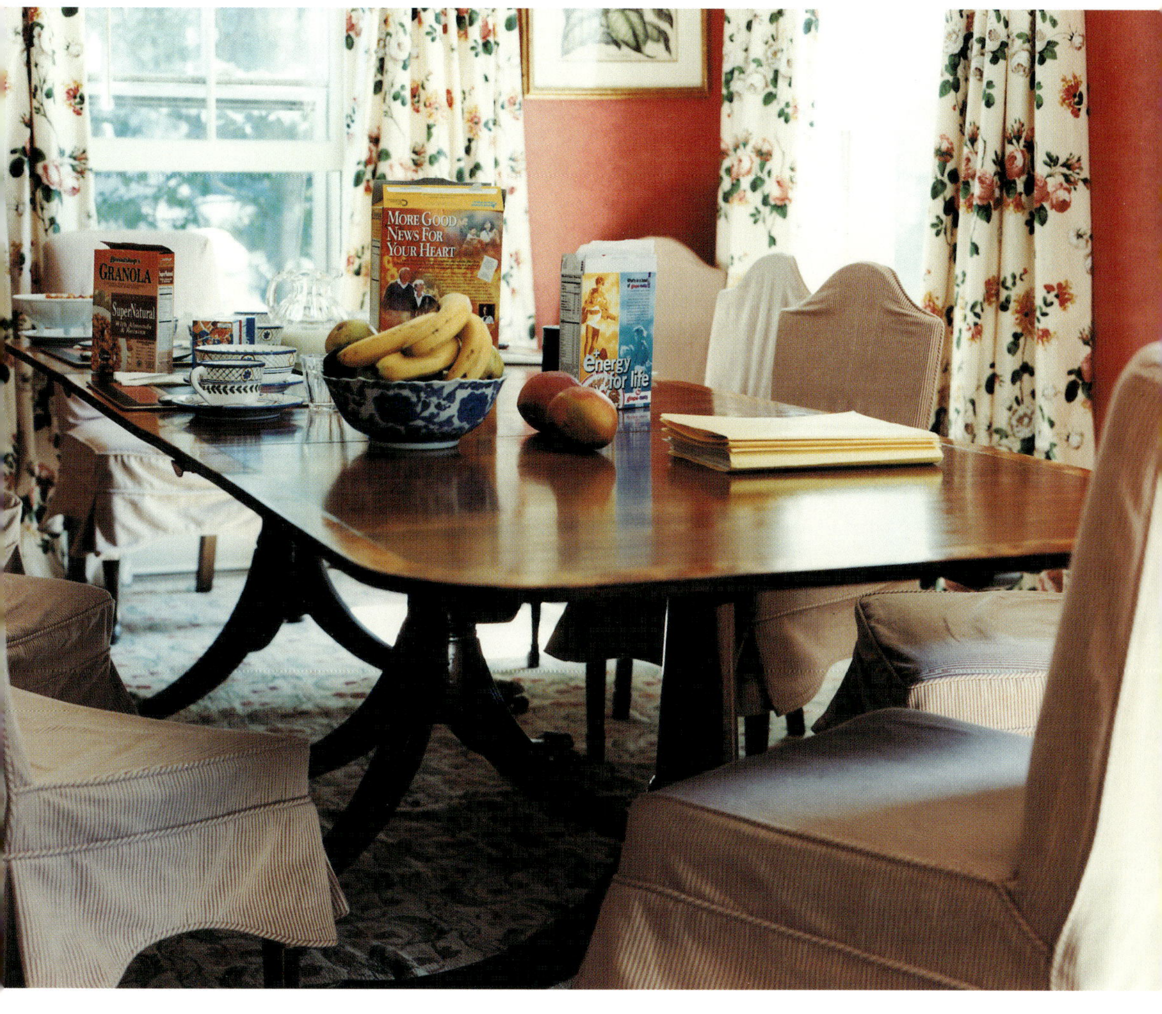

GRANOLA
SuperNatural
With Almonds
& Raisins
MORE GOOD
NEWS FOR
YOUR HEART
energy
for life

GREGG BORDOWITZ

he day I came out, I was sitting with my parents at the kitchen table. My sister was upstairs watching TV. My parents must have sensed that I was going to broach some serious topic, because if I weren't I would have been upstairs watching TV too. Throughout my life, members of my family always occupied the same seats at the kitchen table. I sat on the same side as my mother, facing my stepfather. On this day, I occupied the seat my sister usually sat in, facing my mother, my stepfather to the left of me. I told them. I said there was something they should know and accept about me if they expected me to include them in my life. I am gay. My mother burst into tears. My stepfather got up to pace. My mother couldn't stop crying for about two hours. My stepfather surprised me with his response. It was OK as far as he was concerned. Attempting to quiet my mother, he appealed to her to look at the bright side: "Linda, Linda, look. Come on, stop crying. Look, he didn't kill anybody, and he's not a drug addict," he said emphatically looking at me for reassurance. At least I hadn't killed anybody. At some point my sister came downstairs to see what was happening. Looking at my mother, who was trying to contain her sobs, she asked what was wrong. I looked at her and said that I had just told our parents that I am gay. She started crying, too, like she'd been cued. I thought to myself, the whole thing feels scripted. My sister must have felt implicated. Maybe this meant she was queer. Maybe she thought she'd have to tell people at school. I still don't know, we haven't talked about it since. Through time my parents have come to deal with it. They're now aware that I have this infection, although their response to learning this was much less emotional than my coming out. I thought it should have been more painful. I don't think they realized the implications, and I gave them a very optimistic picture. I didn't admit to them that I fear my own death in the next few years. I lied to them. Told them it was like diabetes. I can keep it under control. I fed them the bullshit I'd love to hear someone else tell me, and the things I knew they were capable of hearing. I'm tired of representing the situation in ways that take care of the needs of the listener.

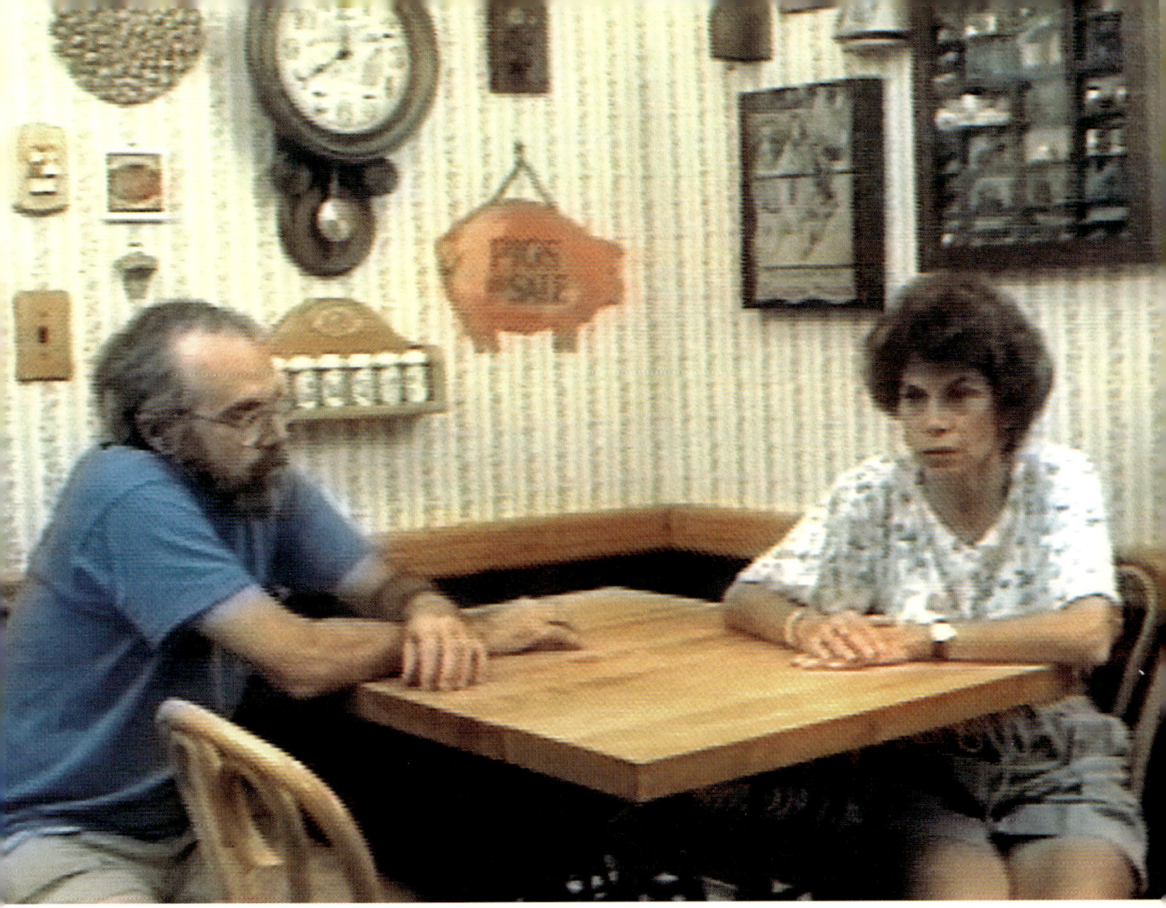

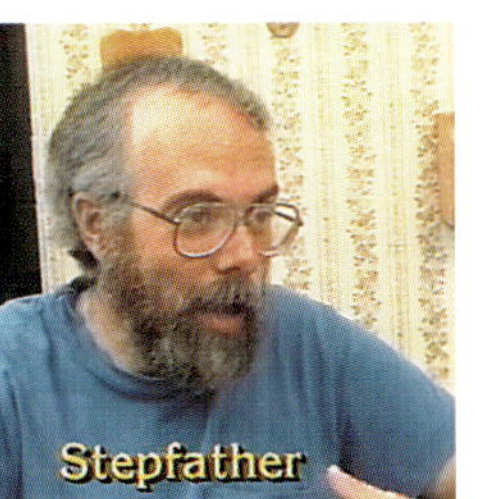

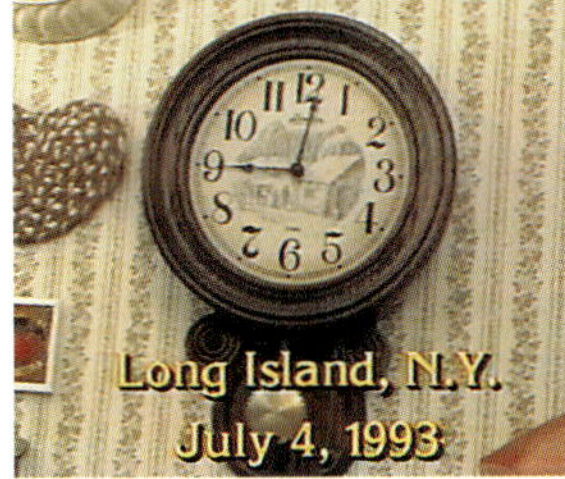

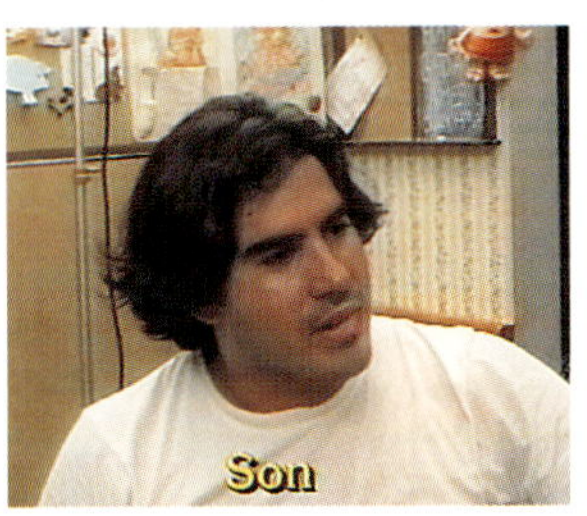

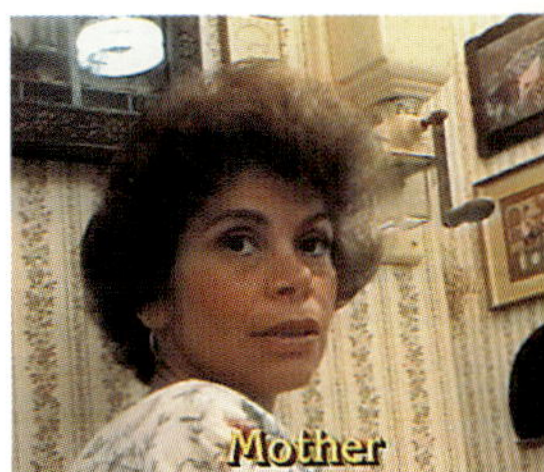

Stills
Fast Trip, Long Drop, 1993

Courtesy of the artist

Text
Excerpt from "Dense Moments," *Uncontrollable Bodies: Testimonies of Identity and Culture*, ed. Rodney Sappington and Tyler Stallings (Seattle: Bay Press, 1994), p. 38

Used with the author's permission

DILLER + SCOFIDIO

Indigestion condenses an archetypal film noir narrative into a terse exchange between two characters of ambiguous relation across a dinner table. It is presented in two electronically linked modes: an interactive video and a virtual environment. Systems of choice are offered to lure the subject into an interrogation of the democratic aspirations of interactive technologies and to critique reductive binaries such as masculine/feminine, high class/low class, fact/fiction, and real/virtual.

The video consists of a dining scene projected onto a horizontal screen/table that a viewer can join as a guest. There, a touch screen offers character replacements from a variety of gender and class stereotypes. The narrative remains continuous at any switch point though nuanced by differences of character.

In the virtual environment, a participant using a Polhemus motion-sensing device can navigate in real time through the computer-generated, magnified space of the same dinner table. The image is split onto two large screens on opposite sides of the room for 3-D viewing. The mobile and magnified viewpoint across this mega-landscape will reveal a micro-drama played out in the details.

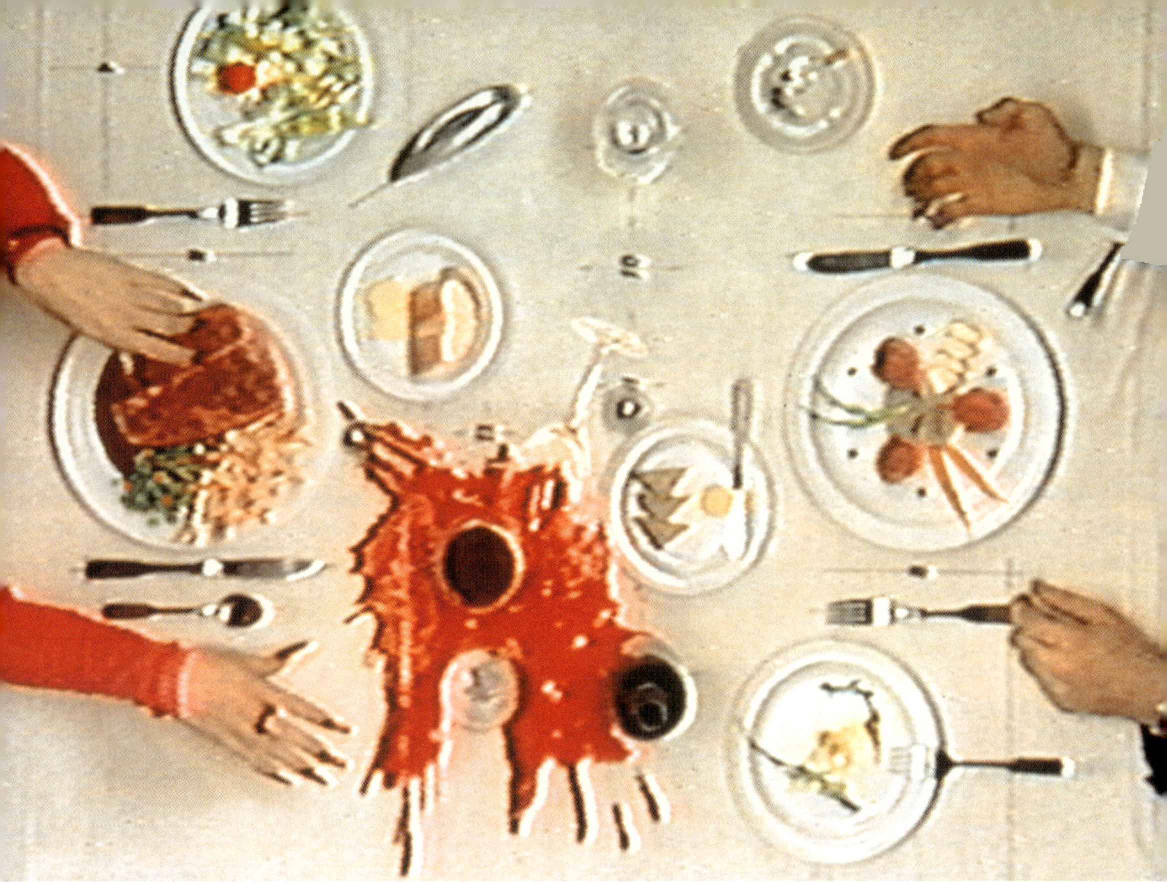

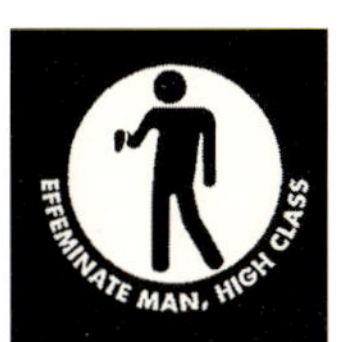

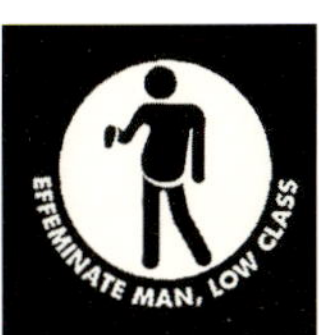

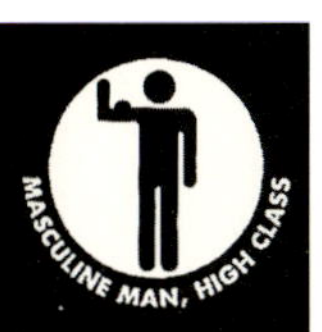

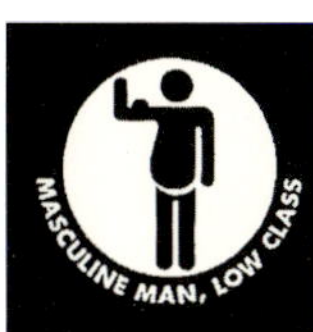

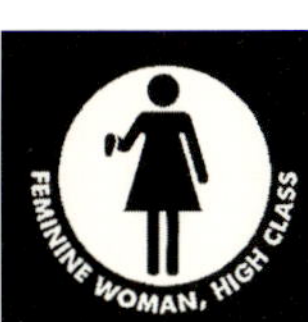

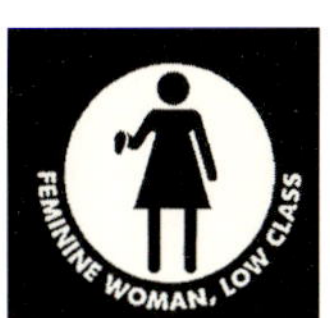

INDIGESTION, 1995

Interactive installation in collaboration with
the Banff Centre for New Media Research;
script by Douglas Cooper, voices directed
by Marianne Weems

Courtesy of the artists

ANN HAMILTON

the first room...water precedes words, the hum of spinning liquid,
150 vortexes scoring the beeswax walls, from a megaphone of flax,
twisted and braided, a mouthpiece invites speech,
speech stills the spin of the water, blocking the end of the horn,
the image of an ear flooding with water

the middle room...below an algae encrusted waterline,
the sound of crickets, a table surfaced with flowing water,
a figure stands with fingers absorbed through holes in the table,
a heavy canvas suit ends in a formless cord

the last room...walls dark with a surface of rubbed graphite,
the floor, a bed of text, ten tons of linotype, a buoy etched with
the lines of a phrenology chart, tied to the canvas tail,
on the wall, a stick figure jerked by turning calipers

the capacity of absorption,
DECEMBER 13, 1988–FEBRUARY 26, 1989
Installation at the Temporary Contemporary/
The Museum of Contemporary Art, Los Angeles

Courtesy of the artist

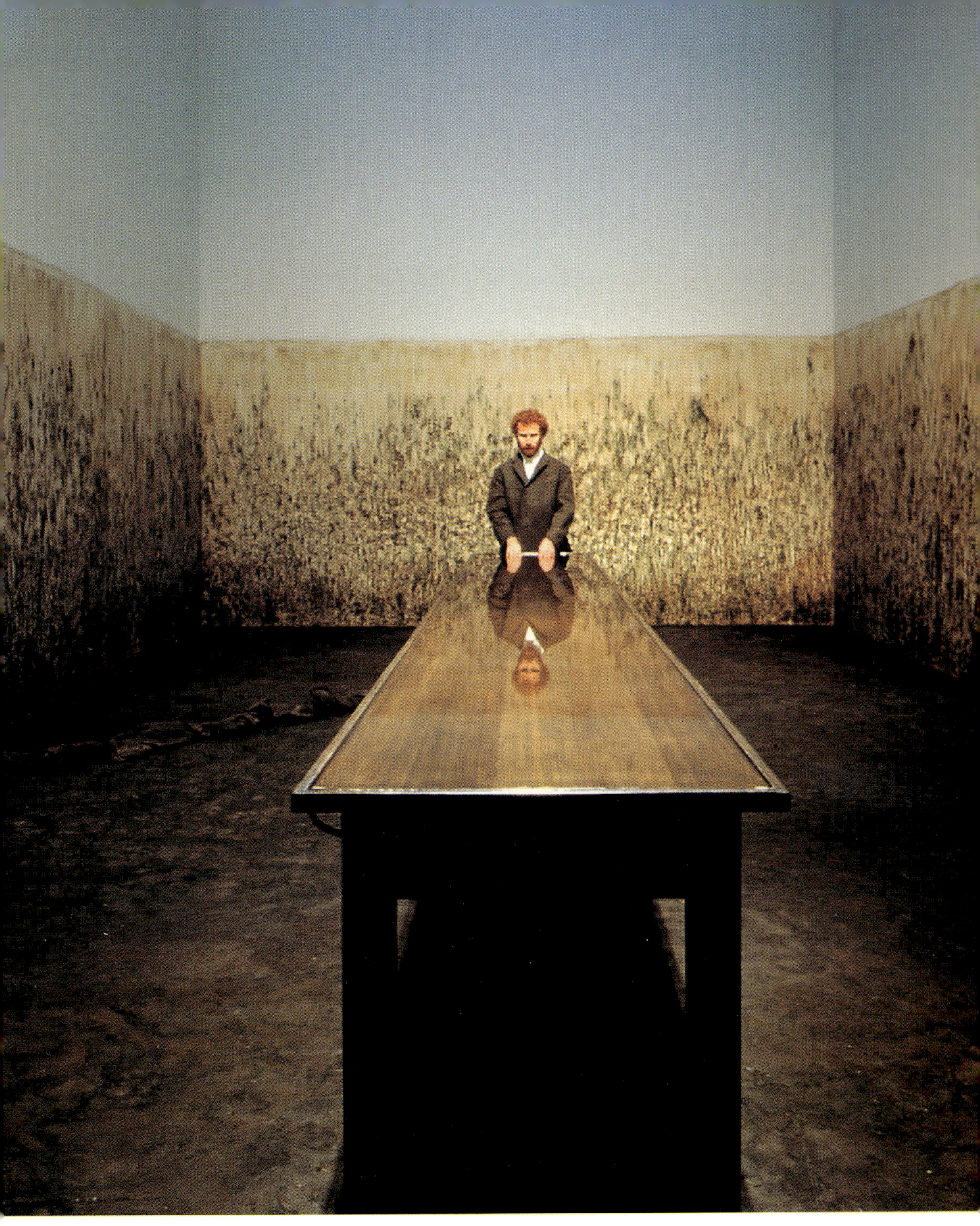

MARTIN SCORSESE

Narrator (V. O.)

The van der Luydens stood above all the city's families. They dwelled in a kind of super-terrestrial twilight, and dining with them was at best no light matter. Dining there with a Duke who was their cousin was almost a religious solemnity.

Narrator (V. O.)

The real thing was never said or done or even thought, but only represented by a set of arbitrary signs. These signs were not always subtle, and all the more significant for that. The refusals were more than a simple snubbing. They were an eradication.

Narrator (V. O.)

When the van der Luydens chose, they knew how to give a lesson.

*CUT to the **CENTERPIECE** of the dinner table. We **DOLLY IN ON** an epergne laden with **FLOWERS** and **CASCADING WATER**.*

*On **THE** dolly in, **MUSIC SWELLS** and **SOUNDS** of **DINNER CONVERSATION** become more prominent.*

*CUT to **EXTREME CLOSE-UP** of an individual **ICE MOLD** on a guest's plate. (This signifies a change in the dinner course.)*

*CUT TO a direct **OVERHEAD SHOT** of the whole long table in the grand room.*

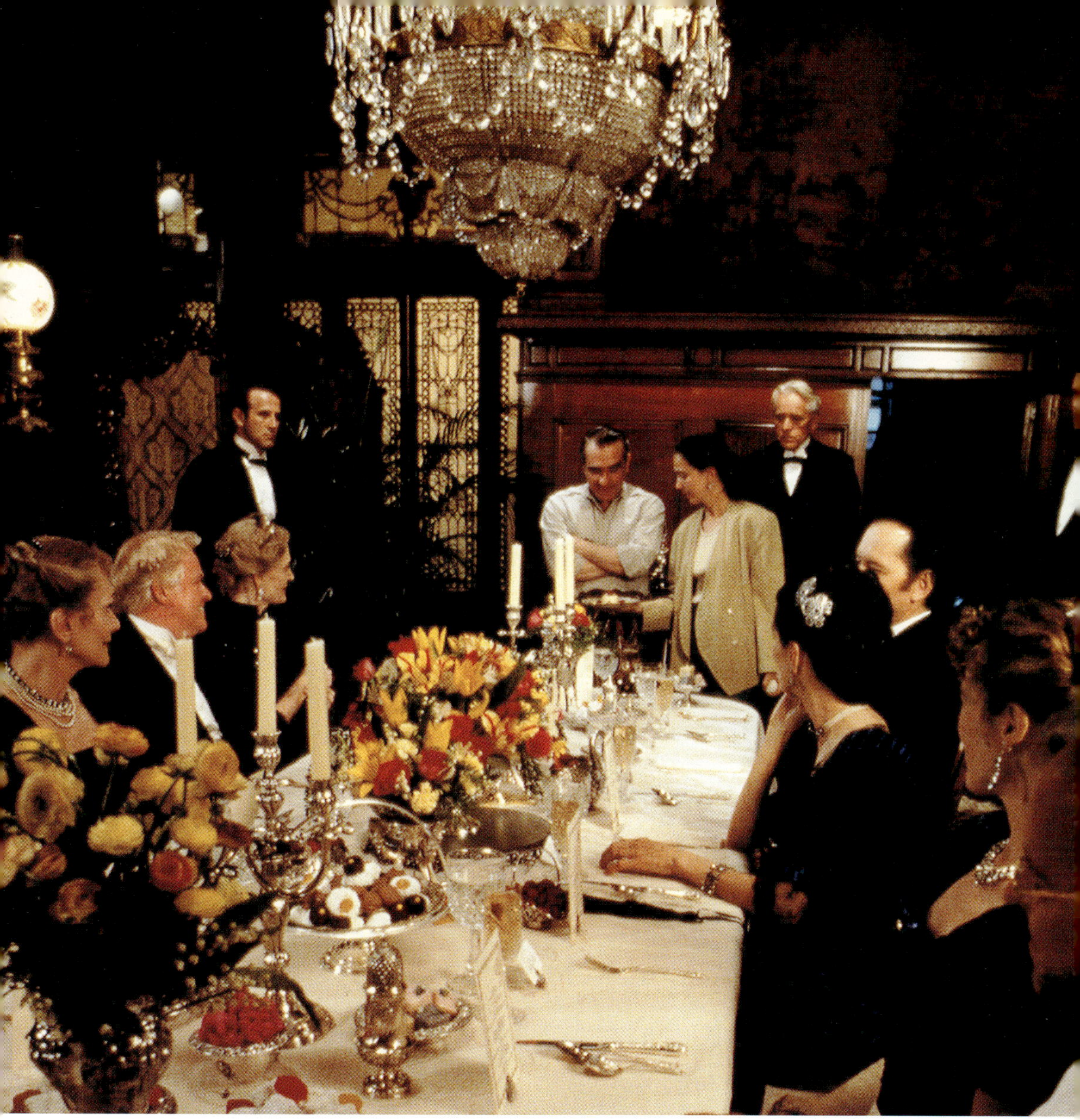

THE AGE OF INNOCENCE, 1993

TEXT
Excerpts from *The Age of Innocence: The Shooting
Script/Screenplay and Notes by Martin Scorsese
and Jay Cocks* (New York: Newmarket Press, 1995),
p. 23, p. 20, p. 24

PHOTO
Courtesy of the Scorsese Archive

ALLAN WEXLER

92

Set T: Acrylic on Photographs (B), 1989
Acrylic on photographs on plywood

Courtesy of the artist

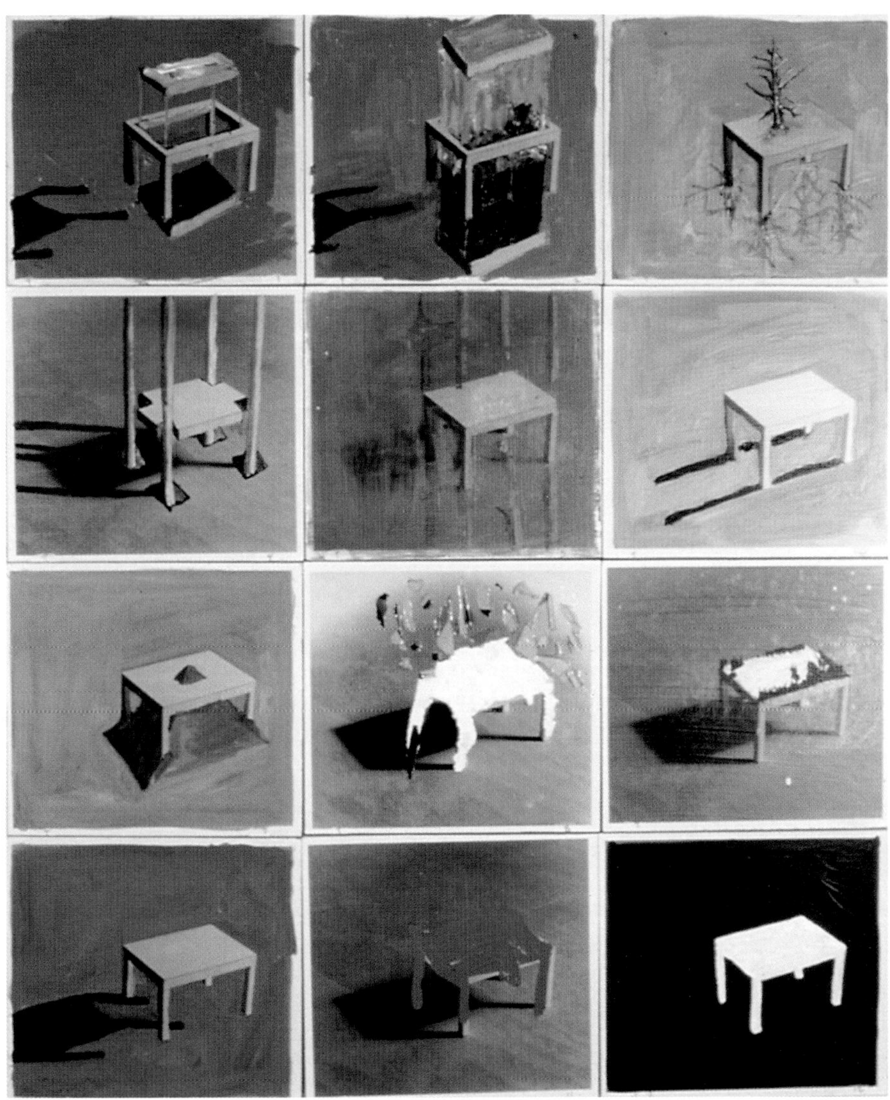

VITO ACCONCI

The entrance to the enclosed room is walled off, and the outside of the room is painted black: the room becomes an object within the overall space—an object loaded with the memory that there's a room inside. Alongside the room, running through the corridor, is a wooden plank forty feet long and two feet wide, a plank that changes function: it starts by settling into the room as a table, eight stools on either side—but it doesn't stop there, it continues toward the window, extends out the window and becomes a diving board.

The gallery, then, is used as a meeting place. Hanging down above the plank—at the point where table turns into diving board—is a set of speakers: a clock ticks, my voice calls the meeting to order: one sentence keeps coming back, "Now that we know we failed…": this is a meeting at the edge: this is like a game of musical chairs, not everybody has a place here. There's something off to the side, there are "skeletons" in the closet: from inside the black room come muffled voices, the sounds of a crowd—this is something we can fall back on, this is something that keeps nagging at us. When the crowd dies out, one voice stands alone, at the table: each of us has a different answer. By this time the clock is ticking again: the meeting begins one more time: "Now that we're back where we started…"

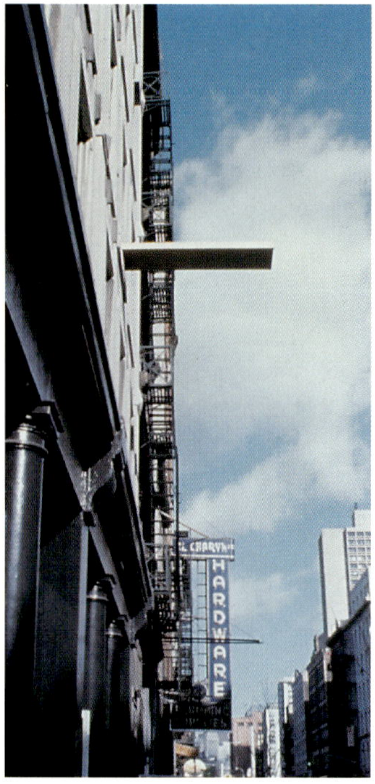

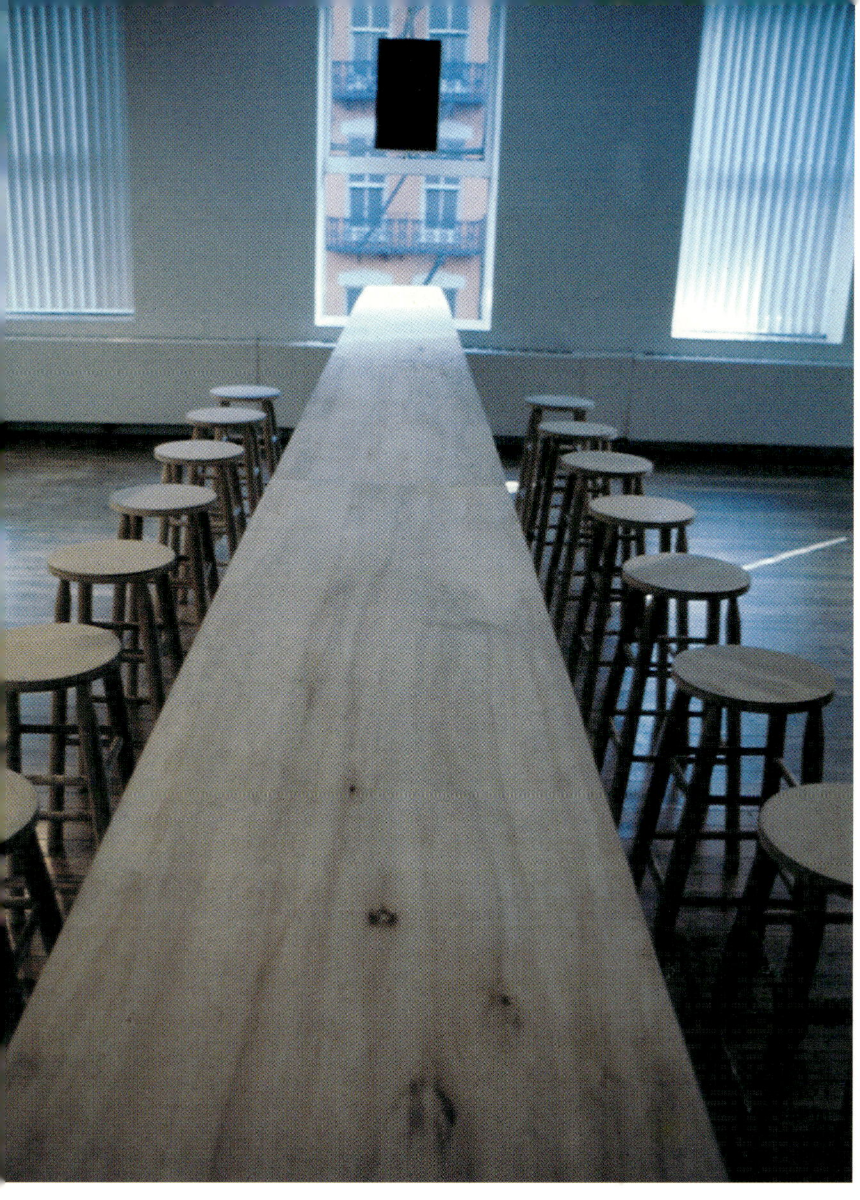

Where We Are Now (Who Are We Anyway?), NOVEMBER 1976
Installation at Sonnabend Gallery, New York

Courtesy of the artist

TEXT
Excerpt from artist's statement

MACK SCOGIN AND MERRILL ELAM

THESE TABLES ARE THE
TABLES IN OUR HOUSE, 1998
Composite exposures

Courtesy of Scogin Elam and Bray Architects, Inc.

these tables are the tables in our house

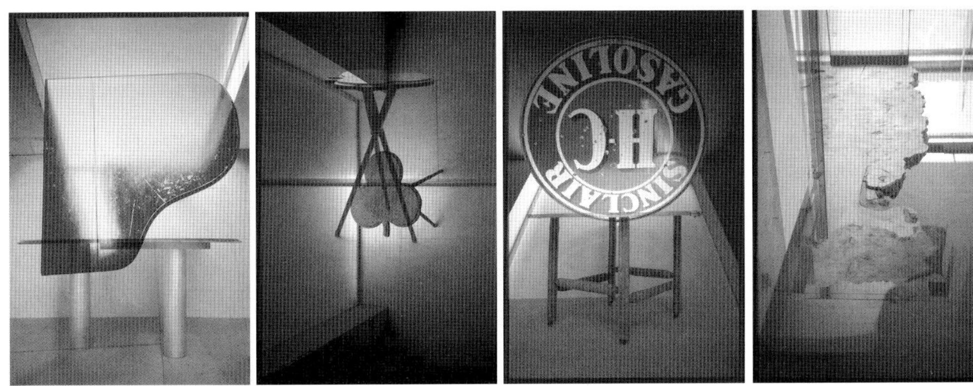

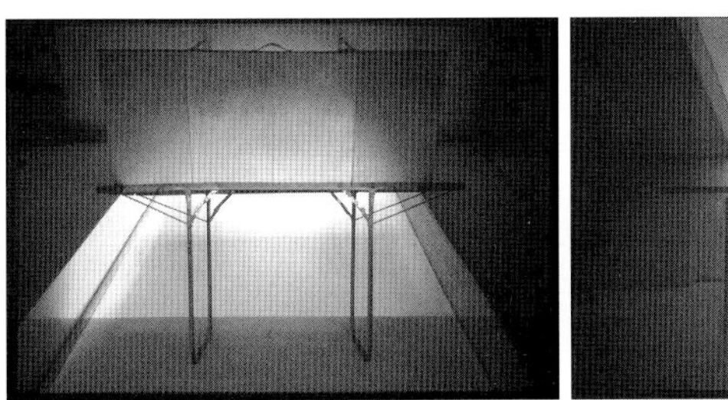

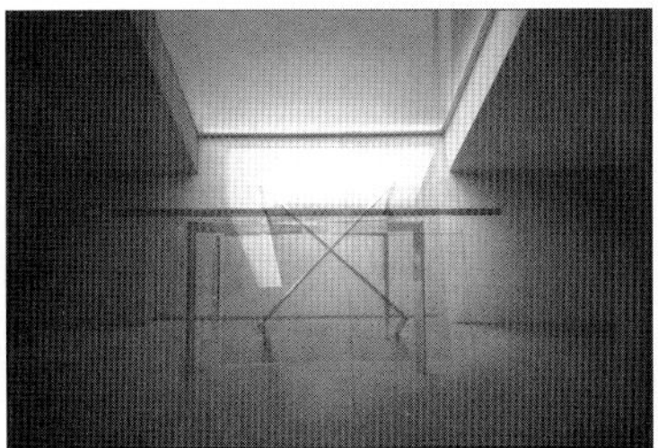

JEFFREY KIPNIS

Y: Pass that, man; ow, dammit. Watch what you're doing, will you? You burnt the fuckin' table.

Hey man, do you ever think about tables; I mean, think how much fuckin' bullshit surrounds tables. D'you know that for like years, the Americans and the North Vietnamese debated about the shape of the negotiating table and the seating arrangements before they would even start the peace talks. And so did Fisher and Spastik, or whatever that guy's name was, before they played chess.

M: Who?

Y: Boris somebody. Russian who lost the chess championship to Bobby Fisher. My Russian History 841 teacher is convinced that Fisher's winning triggered the eventual downfall of the Soviet Union and the end of the Cold War. Claims she can prove it using Catastrophe Theory, Chaos Theory, butterfly effect and stuff like that. Even traces it to the design of the table and chess set. Just got a big grant. Who the hell ever thought you'd have to study like radical mathematics in a history class.

M: You know, when you mention that stuff about tables, it makes me thank god for the big bang.

Y: No shit. Like, when it comes to the big bang, who else?

M: No, I mean it, seriously.

Y: ....?

M: Well, look at it this way. First of all you got to realize that the big bang was real, I mean really real, not just some story about long, long ago. Physically fucking real. We can hear it; watch it on TV. Did you know that the fuzz you used to see between TV channels before they started covering it up with a blue screen was the big bang? So, when you thought your dad was just sleeping when he sat in front of the TV with his beer all night, he was actually watching the big bang in real time.

Y: Get the fuck out of here, and...?

M: Well, that means everything, absolutely everything, every object, every person, every thought, every feeling has a history, evolved in history. Like this: they weren't around at the big bang, now they're around, so somewhere along the way, they went from not being here to being here. All the philosophical bullshit about the existential tableness of the table, the phenomenology, the transcendent essence of the table, or any of that shit must come to grips with the fact that it evolved in time and continues to evolve.

Y: Yeah, so?

M: Well, now, consider the material flows that generate that evolution. First the big bang turns into hydrogen and helium gas; then these collapse into stars, then the stars cook the helium into the heavier elements like carbon and shit that make up tables, then the stars blow up spreading those elements, then the gasses from blown up stars collapse into planets, then water comes along, then life, then wood, then people, then people meet wood, then tables, then sitting around tables, then changing the shape of tables to effect what happens when you sit around them—like, the knights of the round table and shit—then buying and selling tables, eating on tables, fucking on tables, cutting people up on tables, then changing the tables' materials, the shape of their parts, thinking about tables and talking about them, and so on and so on. The catch is, is that each step in these vast materialist flows and processes along the way generates a diagram, and that all of the billions of diagrams generated in the evolutionary history of the table condenses into and is recapitulated by each specific table like a fantastic vortex. Each table, in turn, keeps that evolution going; every individual table is a potential new type of table or even a new type of something else. A table is like a fruit fly is like a tornado.

Y: That's awesome!...Let's go get something to eat.

..., 1998

DAVID LANG

I am writing this on my computer, which takes up the whole of my work table.

It used to be that all the best composers wrote music for the table. It wasn't music for the work table or the coffee table, but for the dinner table; it was music to be played while other people ate. The best composers go where the best work is, and writing background music for dining aristocrats was considered good work. It was its own entire genre of music in the 18th century, with its own rules and traditions and its own musicological designation in German, *tafelmusik*. By design, this music couldn't be very interesting, or lively, or loud. The music for the table couldn't interfere with the diners seated around it.

A dinner table can be something personal, something intimate or casual, something that's ours, but it only becomes personal to those who have been invited to the dinner. To composers writing for other diners, such as Handel or Telemann, Mozart or Haydn, "the table" was a well-paid insult, a reinforcement of a hierarchy, a gig.

It is the idea of the intimate table that plays a role in more recent music. From his fluxus period, La Monte Young's *Poem for Chairs, Tables and Benches* drags furniture around the room, creating the possibility of making music out of the ordinary and the personal. Philip Glass's first experiment with repetition was in a piece called *One + One*, in which a solo performer drums his or her fingers on an amplified tabletop.

I once wrote a piece for percussion ensemble in which the performers construct a table and chairs on stage. The piece is over when all the players are seated around the table, staring at the audience, sitting in the chairs they have just built.

Music for the Table, 1998

Text
Courtesy of the author

Image
Excerpt from *Tafelmusik geteilt in drei Produktionen von Georg Philipp Telemann*, (Leipzig: Ernst Eulenburg, n.d.), p. 1

Musique de Table

3me Production

1.

a. Ouverture

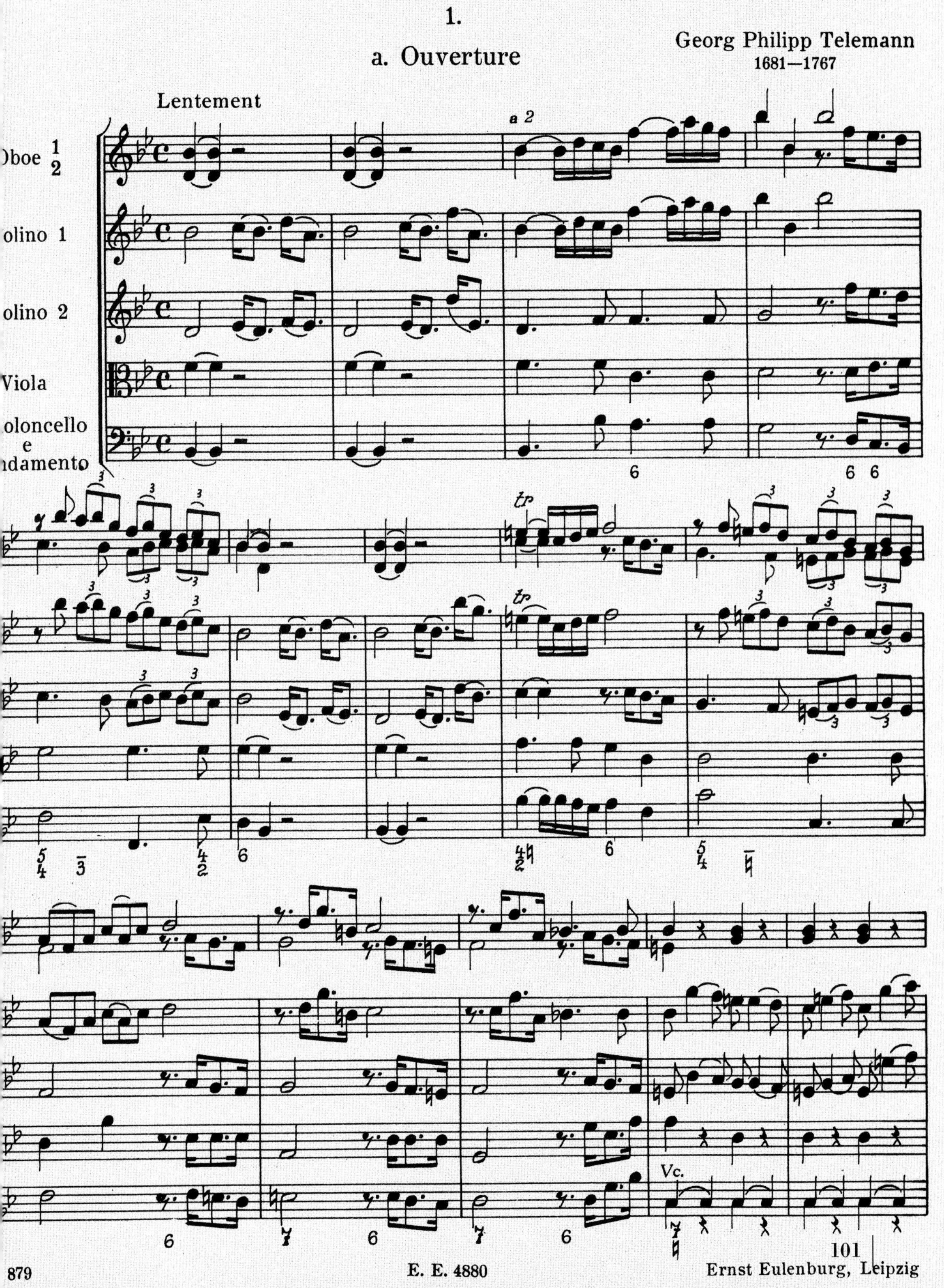

HOLLY BRUBACH

TABLE 1

When I was a little girl, a table was for sitting under. The dining table was modern, in blond wood with a pronounced grain. The ceiling in those days was too far above me. I needed reassurance that the sky wouldn't fall on my head.

TABLE 2

I did my homework seated on the floor at the coffee table in the living room. My parents kept urging me to get up and sit in a chair. But it was the sixties, and my generation sat on the floor, as a way of expressing solidarity with those who had no chairs. The coffee table was long and narrow, with four removable glass panels, each about a foot square. The panels, turned upside down, could function as trays. I don't remember my parents ever using them that way, not even for parties. Still, I thought it was a nifty concept.

TABLE 3

When I was a teenager, we moved into a new house and replaced the blond wood dining table with a Louis XVI replica—the top walnut, the base carved and painted white. This signified our upward progress in the community.

TABLES, 1998

Courtesy of the author

TABLE 4

As a recent college graduate in New York, I became the beneficiary of spare furniture from my grandmother's house, including a mahogany dining table with Queen Anne legs. During my childhood, it had resided in the upstairs parlor, where we used it for wrapping Christmas presents. My cousin Glenn, Jr., otherwise known as "Bud," had carved his nickname into the top with a pocketknife. Years later, sitting at the table, I embarked on my career as a freelance writer.

TABLE 5

A friend, visiting in Paris for a weekend, was shocked to find me picnicking on the floor of my empty dining room and resolved to buy me a table at the flea market. We settled on a Louis XVI table that seats six, with a carved green-painted base and a marble top. When it was delivered, I thought, This is the real thing of which my mother's was the copy.

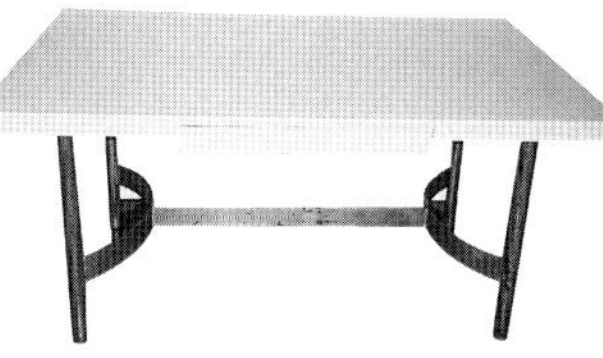

TABLE 6

Two years ago, after hip replacement surgery, I came home to my new loft. Construction had been completed while I was in the hospital; my only furniture was a bed and three patio chairs. I would be housebound, on crutches, for six weeks. My friend David, an interior designer, called. "Can I do anything for you?" he asked. Come to think of it, yes, I replied and asked him to loan me a table. Later that day, he sent over something his firm had put into storage in the basement: a schizophrenic orphan with a gilded metal base in the style of 1940s French furniture and a faux-granite plastic-laminate top that takes after 1970s American kitchen counters. Sitting at the table, I wrote a children's book in which everyday objects have not only personalities but souls, and a boy befriends them.

LYNNE COHEN

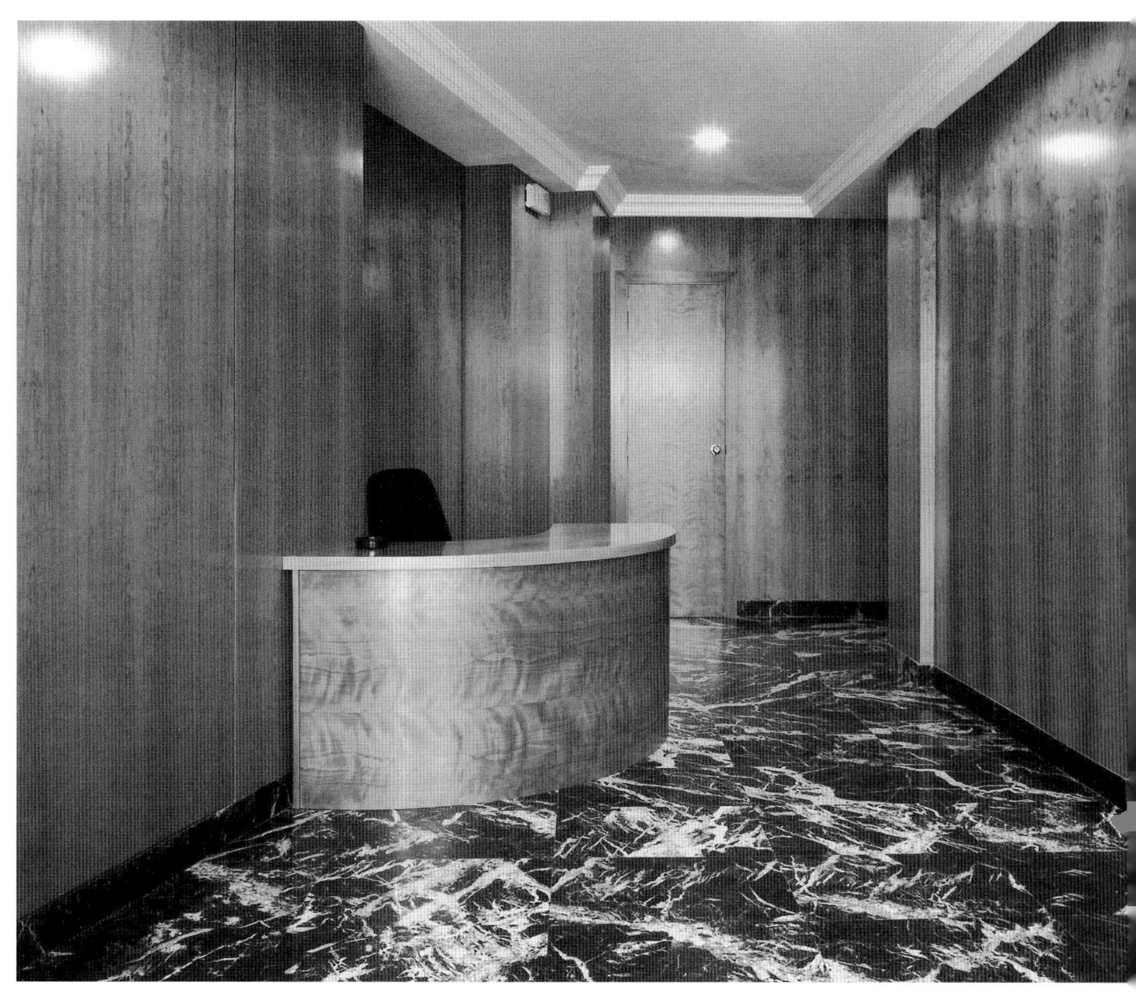

RANDALL KENAN

They were in the little dining room off from the kitchen when he finally told her. He paced about, motioning with his hands.

She just sat there, staring down. Feeling nothing. Maybe. Or just plain tired.

"I can't do it anymore, Sandra," he said.

Sandra said nothing. Slowly, she moved her hand over the oilcloth, steadying herself.

"I don't care what your family says about me," he said. "I don't care. I can't…I'm not…I've got to…"

She might have asked Dean about the children. But the idea that he would come up with some sleazy nonsense only made her feel a wave of nausea. Sandra put her head down.

Dean stopped behind her. She could feel the tension in the air; without seeing them, she knew he was clenching and unclenching and clenching his fists. He did that when he was angry. "Did you hear me? I'm leaving."

Sandra raised her head. "Then go."

He stood there for the amount of time it takes a frying egg to turn white and walked from the room.

Sandra reached out and caressed it, and remembered. Not so much remembered as allowed a flood of images, past scents, past sights, to overtake her, to fill in the void she was now harboring. Each image evoked something like a feeling. So much took place in this room, upon this very surface. Not merely the food served, or the home-work fretted over, or the cards played, or the beer spilled, or the puzzles arranged. Moments occurred right here. And now, in this instance of illusions-shattered, of dreams-wrecked and of a heart-frozen, these fragments of time seemed to simmer before her, behind her eyes, and she could only hold onto it, to find some strength.

WHERE SHE SITS, 1998

Courtesy of the author

She had inherited this very one from her great-grandmother. Made of pine, by whom she did not know, it had been oiled, dented, dusted, polished, chipped, varnished, battered, peed upon, burned, broken, mended, hammered, nailed or some such for decades. If it could feel she knew she'd feel the way it felt now...

"Sandra? Damn it!...Where is my..."

The first true memory of her grandmother had been watching her across this expanse, at the other end, as the silver-haired lady smiled and sliced with pride a piping hot blueberry pie. No, child, wait for it to cool. And so many mornings, days, nights with her mother at that same end: What you doing out so late? Sandra! An A in math! Now that's good. Girl, don't you ever raise your voice at me. I'll knock the taste out your mouth! You heard about Uncle William, didn't you?...

"Sandra, can't find my..."

As if he actually expected her to come in there and help him to pack, to leave; as if any of this fault rested on her shoulders; as if she were expected to go along to get along; as if she would be unreasonable to go into the kitchen, get a butcher's knife and chop him into seventeen billion little pieces.

She ran her hand out and against it again, against its smooth flatness, as if to absorb some of its stolid solidity.

Here, she served him the first take of her cooking: Catfish, greens, mashed potatoes, corn bread; here, she told her mother she was to wed the man who made her legs feel like overcooked spaghetti, and her heart feel like butter. Here, she tended him, listened to his tales of boring sales meetings and petty office feuds, and where he entertained his buddies (when not in front of the TV); here, where she feed and consoled and interrogated first one, then two daughters; here, where she slowly watched the shoals of her marriage erode, grain by grain.

O', if it could talk...

"Sandra." He stood in the door. She didn't want to look up at him. She had nothing to say.

"Good bye."

She did not look up, as he turned, wordless, and walked down the hall. As the door clicked behind him, she held fast: He may go, but some things would remain. A part, a piece, a fixture, a witness. Even now.

GUILLERMO KUITCA

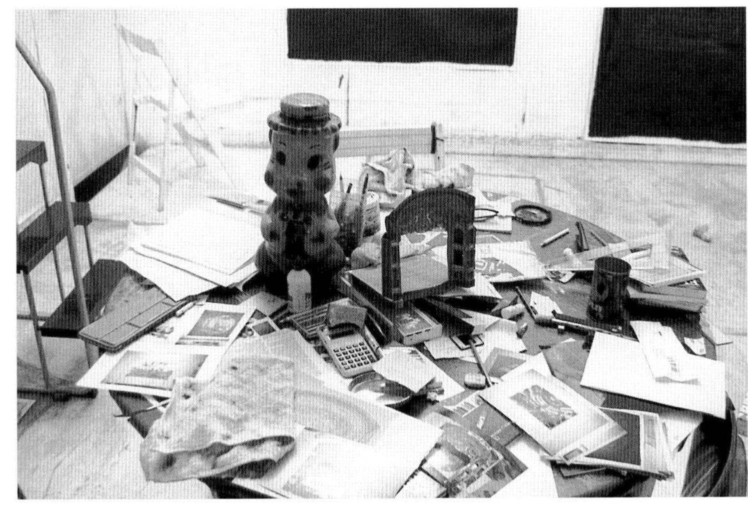

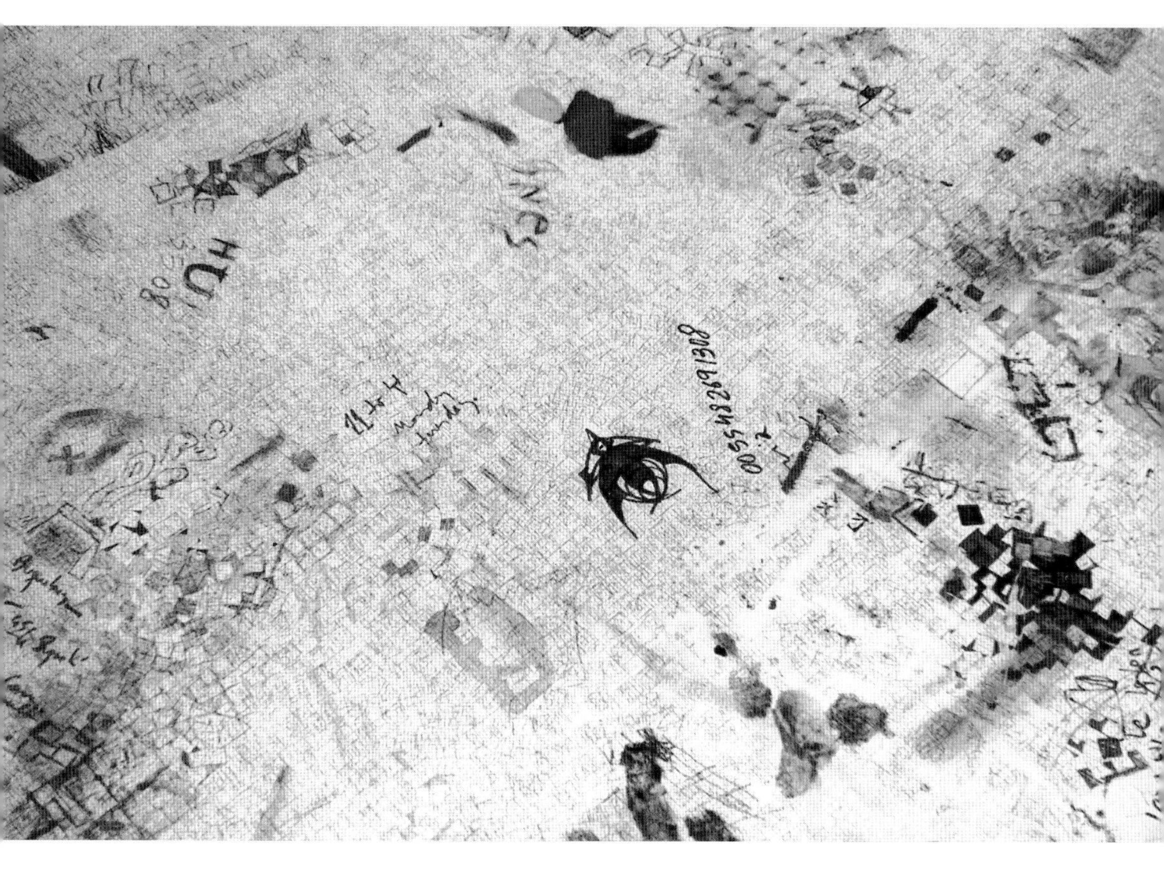

Diary Tables

Left
Diary Table (Studio View),
April 17, 1998–the present

Above
Diary Table (Detail),
November 26, 1997–April 16, 1998

Courtesy of the artist and Sperone Westwater

RENNY RAMAKERS

This side table is one of the results of the "Dry Tech" project set up by Droog Design in 1995. The project was done in collaboration with the Aviation and Space Laboratory of Delft University of Technology, the aim being to combine rough-and-ready low-tech aesthetics with high-tech materials. The designers set up to work along artisanal and intuitive lines. Marcel Wanders' transparant tables have been made by hardening Swiss lace with resin.

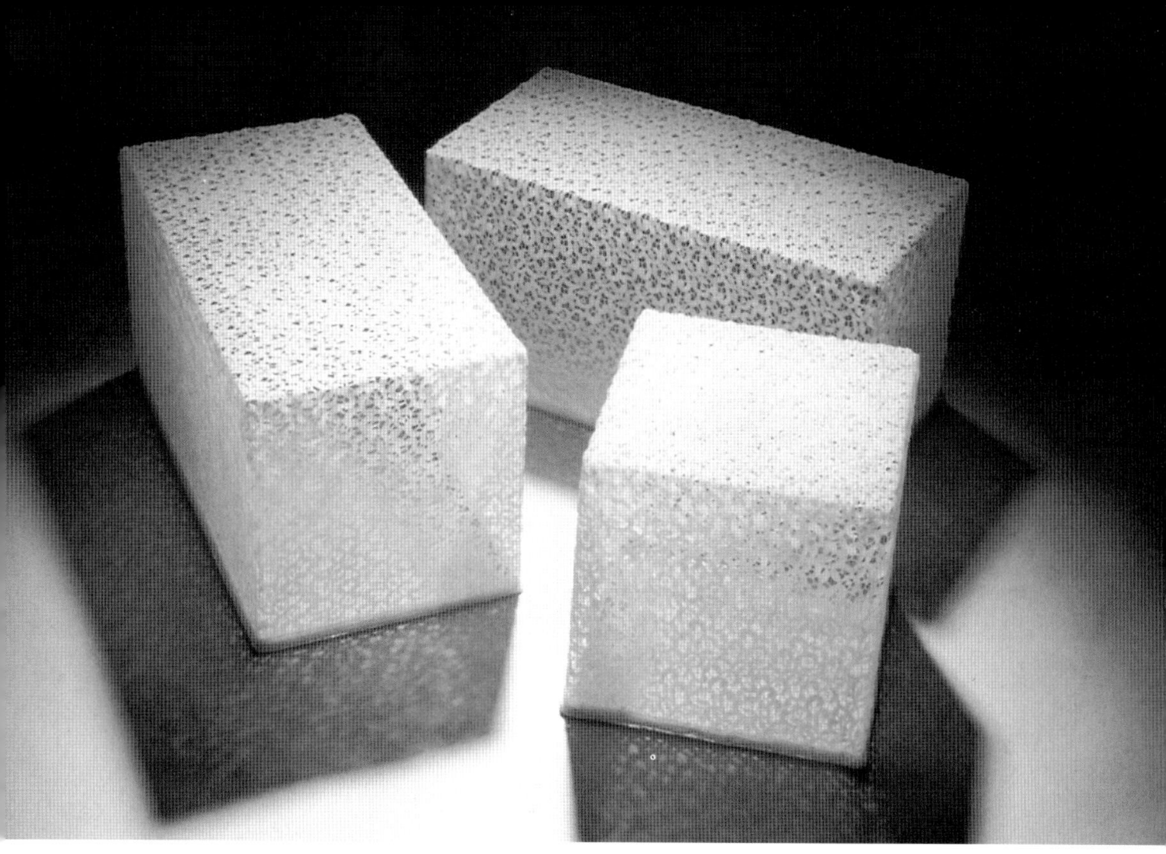

LACE TABLE, 1997
Marcel Wanders for Droog Design

Courtesy of Renny Ramakers

Vɪᴛᴏ Aᴄᴄᴏɴᴄɪ's work has encompassed fiction and poetry, performances, film and video projects, installations, participatory sculpture, architecture, landscape architecture, and furniture design. Since the late 1980s, he has worked with a group of architects as Acconci Studio, designing projects for public spaces such as plazas, parks, and building lobbies. Recent and current projects include an indoor park for the Philadelphia airport and a seating system for a subway station in the Bronx. Acconci Studio is based in Brooklyn, New York.

Tɪɴᴀ Bᴀʀɴᴇʏ, a photographer based in New York City and Watch Hill, Rhode Island, has participated in numerous solo and group exhibitions in the United States and abroad, including solo exhibitions at The Museum of Modern Art in New York and the International Museum of Photography at George Eastman House in Rochester. She is best known for her piercing images of the family and other social institutions.

Gʀᴇɢɢ Bᴏʀᴅᴏᴡɪᴛᴢ is a video/film maker and writer whose works include *Fast Trip, Long Drop*, an experimental film about living with AIDS; *A Cloud in Trousers*, an adaptation of a poem by Vladimir Mayakovski; and *The Suicide*, a feature film adaptation (filmed at the Wexner Center) of a play by Nicolai Erdman. He is on the faculty of the Film Department of the School of the Art Institute of Chicago.

Hᴏʟʟʏ Bʀᴜʙᴀᴄʜ has written about design, architecture, dance, and fashion. She is the author of *Girlfriend: Men, Women, and Drag*, to be published in the spring of 1999 by Random House. The former Style Editor of the *New York Times Magazine*, she now works for Prada, the Italian fashion house, as director of its home collection. She lives in Milan and New York.

Lʏɴɴᴇ Cᴏʜᴇɴ ɪs a photographer who has exhibited widely in North America and Europe. Her work is ironic and disquieting, loaded with references to art both past and present. She currently lives and works in Ottawa, Ontario. Her photographs were featured in *Evidence: Photography and Site*, a touring exhibition organized by the Wexner Center in 1997, and its accompanying catalogue.

Eʟɪᴢᴀʙᴇᴛʜ Dɪʟʟᴇʀ and Rɪᴄᴀʀᴅᴏ Sᴄᴏғɪᴅɪᴏ are cofounders of Diller + Scofidio, an interdisciplinary studio working at the intersection of art, architecture, and the performing arts. The two live and work in New York City. They often create installations for galleries and museums or for public sites and are also involved in architectural commissions, multimedia theater, electronic media, and print. Elizabeth Diller is Associate Professor of Architecture at Princeton University. Ricardo Scofidio is Professor of Architecture at Cooper Union.

Aɴɴ Hᴀᴍɪʟᴛᴏɴ is an artist best know for her large-scale multimedia installations. She has participated in more than sixty solo and group exhibitions since 1981 and will represent the United States at the 1999 Venice Biennale. She was the recipient of a Wexner Center Residency Award in visual arts for 1994–95; her residency culminated in the touring exhibition *the body and the object: Ann Hamilton 1984–1996* and an accompanying catalogue and CD-ROM project. She currently lives in Columbus, Ohio.

Rᴀɴᴅᴀʟʟ Kᴇɴᴀɴ is the author of a novel, *A Visitation of Spirits*, and a collection of stories, *Let the Dead Bury Their Dead*. His latest book is *Walking on Water: Black American Lives at the Turn of the Twenty-First Century*. He currently lives in Memphis, Tennessee.

Jeffrey Kipnis is an architectural critic, theorist, and designer. He is Professor of Architecture at the Austin E. Knowlton School of Architecture, The Ohio State University.

Guillermo Kuitca has exhibited his paintings and installations in solo and group exhibitions at venues including Instituto Valenciano de Arte Moderno (IVAM) in Valencia, Spain; The Museum of Modern Art, New York; and the Art Institute of Chicago. A native of Argentina, he currently lives and works in Buenos Aires. The traveling exhibition *Burning Beds: Guillermo Kuitca, A Survey 1982–1994* was organized by the Contemporary Art Foundation, Amsterdam, and premiered at the Wexner Center in 1994.

David Lang is cofounder and co-artistic director of Bang on a Can, an organization dedicated to adventurous new music, and composer-in-residence with the American Conservatory Theater in San Francisco. He has composed commissioned works for the Boston Symphony, the Cleveland Orchestra, the Santa Fe Opera, and choreographer Susan Marshall. A new collaboration with Marshall and a fully staged opera for the Kronos Quartet are among his upcoming projects.

Renny Ramakers is the cofounder of Droog Design in Rotterdam, the Netherlands, and a design critic who has contributed to magazines, newspapers, books, and exhibition catalogues. She was the chief editor of *Industrieel ontwerpen* (Industrial Design) from 1988 to 1993 and of *Items*—the leading Dutch magazine on design, communication, and architecture— from 1993 to 1997.

Mack Scogin and **Merrill Elam** are Principals of Scogin Elam and Bray Architects, Inc., Atlanta, Georgia. The firm's current and recent projects include the Riverdale Branch Library, Riverdale, Georgia; TBS Office Building and Tape Library, Atlanta, Georgia; Law Library, Arizona State University, Tempe, Arizona; Child Development Center, Corning, Incorporated, Corning, New York; Austin E. Knowlton School of Architecture, The Ohio State University; and the reinstallation of the permanent collection of the High Museum of Art.

Martin Scorsese is the director of such films as *Mean Streets, Alice Doesn't Live Here Anymore, Taxi Driver, Raging Bull, The Last Temptation of Christ, GoodFellas, The Age of Innocence,* and *Kundun.* He is also a champion of film preservation and seeks to encourage new talent through his producing efforts. His many honors and awards include the American Film Institute Lifetime Achievement Award and the Wexner Prize, presented by the Wexner Center and The Ohio State University.

Allan Wexler's work blurs the borderlines between sculpture, furniture, and architecture. He has participated in numerous solo and group exhibitions internationally and has taught art and architecture for 25 years, currently in the Department of Architecture at Pratt Institute in New York. Permanent public installations of his work include an "artist's residence" at the Mattress Factory in Pittsburgh; a "picnic area" at the DeCordova Museum in Lincoln, Massachusetts; and a "kitchen" in the Environmental Design Department at Parsons School of Design, New York.

THE COLLECTIONS

Functional objects such as tables and tableware can be found in many different kinds of collections. As examples of decorative arts, crafts, or design, they have entered the collections of encyclopedic and specialized museums of the arts. As artifacts of particular lives or of the material culture of specific times or places, they are found in historic houses and at historical museums and living history sites. The institutions that have cooperated with the Wexner Center by lending tables and tableware for this exhibition reflect much of this broad spectrum of collecting approaches.

The **Brooklyn Museum of Art,** one of the largest art museums in the United States, traces the history of its collections to the founding of the Apprentices Library Association in 1823. The first wing of its current building opened in 1897. In addition to world-renowned collections of ancient Egyptian art and American painting and sculpture, the museum is particularly noted for its extensive and significant collection of decorative arts. The museum was one of the pioneers in presenting decorative arts in period rooms, and it currently has twenty-eight period rooms on display. Additional strengths of its decorative arts collection are furniture, silver, and ceramics. Of particular note for this exhibition are the holdings dating from the mid nineteenth century to the mid twentieth century. The Leon Marcotte table (c. 1865), the Charles Parker Company table (1880), the rustic table (1900–20), the Gilbert Rohde desk (c. 1934), the Kem Weber vanity (1934), and the prototype baby feeding set by Eva Zeisel (c. 1940) are drawn from the museum collection.

The **Museum of Fine Arts, Boston,** founded in 1870, is another of the premier public art museums in the United States, with comprehensive collections spanning the globe and the centuries. Ancient, Asian, and African art, along with American and European painting, are among its many strengths. The museum's holdings of American paintings from the eighteenth and early nineteenth centuries are unparalleled, and its extensive decorative arts collection shows similar strengths. The two earliest tables in this exhibition—the lady's work table (c. 1800) and the game and work table (c. 1820–30)—are from this collection, as are the anonymous inscribed oak table (c. 1880) and the card table from the Tobey Furniture Company (1890–1900).

The collection of **The Museum of Modern Art, New York,** founded in 1929, features paintings, sculptures, drawings, prints, photographs, architectural models and drawings, and objects that trace the development of art from impressionism to the present. In 1932 the museum established the first curatorial department of architecture and design in the world. The design collection of this department ranges far beyond traditional concepts of decorative arts to encompass appliances, tools, and even cars and a helicopter, as well as furniture and tableware. Intended to showcase exemplars of exceptional modern design, the collection includes mass market and industrial products, as well as luxury objects. The nesting coffee table by Frederick Kiesler (1938) and the place setting of *Lifetime* ware (1947) are from this collection.

Compared with these arts institutions, the **Musée des Arts Décoratifs de Montréal** (Montreal Museum of Decorative Arts) is both more specialized and a relative newcomer, founded in 1979 by Liliane and David M. Stewart. Dedicated to collecting and exhibiting international decorative arts and design of the twentieth century, the museum has one of the strongest collections of post-1935 decorative arts in North America. The Noguchi chess table (1947) is from this collection.

The **Henry Ford Museum & Greenfield Village** in Dearborn, Michigan, is the largest indoor/outdoor museum complex in the United States. An emphasis on inventions and innovations links its varied displays on such topics as transportation, communications, agriculture, domestic life, and the life and career of automotive pioneer Henry Ford. Of particular import for the current exhibition is the Edsel B. Ford Design History Center, established in 1986 to support research on the creative processes of industrial design. This specialized collection of objects and archival papers includes the Herman Miller Collection, an extensive selection of furniture and prototypes from the Michigan-based company. The lamp table designed by George Nelson (1947–55), the Eames modular desk (c. 1954), and the Eames stool (1960)—all produced by the Herman Miller Furniture Company—are from this collection. The Shaker table (1850–1860) is also from the collections of the Henry Ford Museum & Greenfield Village.

Several of the ceramic objects exhibited in *On the Table*, including the *Museum* dinner service designed by Eva Zeisel (1942–1945), are from **The Arthur E. Baggs Memorial Library Collection, The Ohio State University.** Housed in the ceramics area of Ohio State's Department of Art, the collection incorporates a research library of books and periodicals, as well as a varied selection of historical clay objects. The ceramics program at the university is one of the oldest in the country, and the collection was assembled over many years as a teaching resource. It is named for Arthur Eugene Baggs, a long-time member of the ceramics faculty; two vases by Baggs in the exhibition are also from the library collection.

Functional objects, whether intended for ongoing use, visual enjoyment, or investment, have attracted the enthusiasm of private collectors perhaps even more than have the fine arts. It may thus be appropriate that this exhibition, more than its predecessors in the *Succession of Collections* series, draws from private as well as public collections. Works exhibited in *On the Table* also have come from several corporate collections and archives and from individual designers, manufacturers, and distributors. These lenders are:

Dale Abrams
Comma
Curvet USA, Inc.
Elliot T. Fishman
Interim Office of Architecture,
    John Randolph and Bruce Tomb
Daven Joy and Park Furniture
Donald Judd Estate
Knoll, Inc.
Knoll Museum
Lenox China Archives, Lenox Brands
Marian and Tom McCollough
Parallel Design Partnership
Richard Schultz
Steve M. Shellabarger

CHECKLIST

This checklist is arranged chronologically, from the earliest work to
the most recent, in two sections: Tables and Tableware. In dimensions,
height precedes width precedes depth or height precedes diameter.

Tables

LADY'S WORK TABLE, c. 1800
Anonymous
African mahogany, satinwood,
silk, and brass fittings
29 x 15¾ x 20 in.
Museum of Fine Arts, Boston;
The M. and M. Karolik Collection of 18th
Century American Arts

GAME AND WORK TABLE, c. 1820–30
Anonymous
Mahogany with inlay, brass fittings
30 x 40¼ x 17 in.
Museum of Fine Arts, Boston;
Gift of William N. Banks and Frank Bemis Fund

TABLE, 1850–60
Anonymous Shaker
Pine
28⅛ x 39¼ x 18½ in.
From the Collections of Henry Ford Museum
& Greenfield Village

TABLE, c. 1865
Leon Marcotte
Ebonized woods, brass, and gilded metal
30½ x 57½ x 37½ in.
Brooklyn Museum of Art;
Gift of the Roebling Society

TABLE, c. 1880
Anonymous
Oak; inscription: "IN THE PLACE WHERE
THE TREE FALLETH, THERE IT SHALL
BE WOODENETHE CLADRASTIS TINCTO
RIA..."
27¾ x 27 x 20 in.
Museum of Fine Arts, Boston;
Gift of Aimeé and Rosamond Lamb

TABLE, 1880
Anonymous, for The Charles Parker Company
Brass, other metals, wood, and fabric
29 x 19 x 17½ in.
Brooklyn Museum of Art;
H. Randolph Lever Fund

CARD TABLE, 1890–1900
Anonymous, for Tobey Furniture Company
Mahogany
29¾ x 36 x 18¼ in.
Museum of Fine Arts, Boston;
Anonymous Gift and Helen and
Alice Colburn Fund

RUSTIC TABLE, 1900–20
Anonymous
Painted twigs with black and gray smoked
decoration, branches, and nails
28¾ x 16¾ x 16¾ in.
Brooklyn Museum of Art;
H. Randolph Lever Fund

TABOURET #558, c. 1910
L. & J. G. Stickley
Oak
17 x 15 x 15 in.
Collection of Marian and Tom McCollough

DESK, c. 1934
Gilbert Rohde, for Troy Sunshade
Company, Troy, OH
Polished and chromed steel, wood,
and black plastic laminate
29 x 42 x 22 in.
Brooklyn Museum of Art;
The Brooklyn Museum Fund

Vanity Table, 1934
Kem Weber, for Lloyd Manufacturing
Company, Manominee, MI
Tubular and chrome-plated steel,
painted wood, and mirror
55 x 33 x 19½ in.
Brooklyn Museum of Art;
Modernism Benefit Fund

Nesting Coffee Table, 1938
Frederick Kiesler
Cast aluminum
9½ x 34 x 25 in.; 9½ x 22 x 16¼ in.
The Museum of Modern Art, New York;
Gift of Carlo M. Grossman and Josie G.
Lindau in memory of their parents, Isobel
and Isidore Grossman

Chess Table, model no. IN 61, 1947
Isamu Noguchi, for Herman Miller
Furniture Company
Ebonized plywood, aluminum, and plastic
19¼ x 33⅞ x 30⁵⁄₁₆ in.
Price in 1948: $158
Musée des Arts Décoratifs de Montréal;
Gift of Jay Spectre, by exchange

Lamp Table, 1947–55
George Nelson, for Herman Miller
Furniture Company
Wood, leather, and fluorescent lamp
47 x19 x 30 in.
Price in 1947: $55
From the Collections of Henry Ford Museum
& Greenfield Village

Modular Desk, Eames Storage Units, c. 1954
Charles and Ray Eames, for Herman Miller
Furniture Company
Wood, laminate, micarta, and chrome-plated
metal
60 x 28 x 29¾ in.
From the Collections of Henry Ford Museum
& Greenfield Village

Dining Table, 1956
Eero Saarinen, for Knoll, Inc.
White cast aluminum, white laminate
42¼ x 28¼ in.
Price in 1998: $1627 (new table)
Courtesy of Knoll, Inc.

Petal Table, 1960
Richard Schultz, for Knoll, Inc.
Metal base, white fused plastic finish,
and redwood top
19 x 16 in.
Price in 1974: $104
Courtesy of Richard Schultz

Stool, from Occasional Tables, 1960
Charles and Ray Eames, for Herman Miller
Furniture Company
Solid walnut
15 x 13 in.
Price in 1961: $108
From the Collections of Henry Ford Museum
& Greenfield Village

Cabriole Leg Table, 1984
Robert Venturi, for Knoll, Inc.
Laminated wood, veneer
28½ x 48 x 48 in.
Price in 1988: $2200
Knoll Museum

Granite Cooktop, 1985
Bruce Tomb
Granite, maple, stainless steel, plastic,
and components: camp stove parts, tank
from salvaged fire extinguisher vessel from
Lockheed Co. Bomber, propane gas
40 x 29 x 29 in.
Collection of Interim Office of Architecture,
John Randolph and Bruce Tomb

Frame Table 68, 1989
Donald Judd
Oak
29½ x 29½ x 29½ in.
Price in 1989: $2250
Collection of the Donald Judd Estate

Hatten **End Table**, 1993
Ehlén Johansson, for IKEA
Acrylic, tubular metal
23 x 15¾ in.
Price in 1998: $39.95

NEA Table 2, 1994
M. Ali Tayar
Molded particleboard base,
hardwood legs, and glass tabletop
15 x 30 x 30 in.
Courtesy of Parallel Design Partnership;
made possible by a National Endowment
for the Arts grant

Side Table 114, 1996
Daven Joy and Trav Ebling, for Park Furniture
Maple, stainless steel, and red neoprene
21 x 16 x 14 in.
Price in 1998: $2265
Courtesy of Daven Joy and Park Furniture

Adult Seat, from *Stones*, 1998
Maya Lin, for Knoll, Inc.
Spray-molded fiberglass-reinforced cement
with integral color, polystyrene filler material,
integral UV stabilized pigmented color, and
UV-retardant water sealer top coating
15 x 27 x 19 in.
Price in 1998: $795
Courtesy of Knoll, Inc.

Sexy Sadie Night Table, 1998
David Khouri, for Comma
MDF, lacquer, acrylic, and fluorescent lamp
27 x 14 x 17 in.
Price in 1998: $2150
Courtesy of Comma

Tri-Spectra, 1998
Karim Rashid, for Zeritalia®
Aluminum, glass sheets colored with
water-based paints, and Colorglass™ System
23⅕ x 34 x 34 in.
Price in 1998: $1499
Courtesy of Curvet USA, Inc.

Tableware

TEA LEAF IRONSTONE CHINA, CHINESE SHAPE
AND OTHERS, 1856–80
Anthony Shaw, et al.
White ironstone with copper luster decoration
Soup tureen, chowder tureen, sauce tureen,
tureen undertrays and ladles, large and small
covered vegetable dishes, six table pitchers,
coffee pot, creamer, sugar bowl, handled cup
and saucer, handless cups and saucers, various
sized mugs, pickle dish, large and small compotes, large and small waste bowls, posset cup,
cup plate, gravy boat, set of four nesting platters, dinner plate, lunch plate, side/salad/bread
plate, small plate, butter pat plate, bone dish,
sauce dish, soup bowl, soup plate, nesting open
vegetable dishes, covered butter dish, egg cups,
male spittoon, and female spittoon (undecorated
white china)
Collection of Dale Abrams

VASE, early 20th century
Anonymous, for Pewabic Pottery, Detroit, MI
Ceramic
3 x 4 x 1½ in.
Collection of Steve M. Shellabarger

VASE, early 20th century
Anonymous, for Rookwood Pottery
Ceramic
8½ x 5½ x 2½ in.
Collection of Steve M. Shellabarger

VASE, c. 1923
Charles Walter Clewell, for Clewell Metal Art,
Canton, OH
Ceramic
8¾ x 6¼ x 2 in.
Collection of Steve M. Shellabarger

VASE, c. 1930
Anonymous, for Muncie Pottery, Muncie, IN
Ceramic
6½ x 6 x 2 in.
Collection of Steve M. Shellabarger

FIESTA JUICE TUMBLERS, 1936
Fredrick Rhead, et al., for Homer Laughlin
China Company, Newell, WV
Ceramic
Set of six
Collection of Steve M. Shellabarger

DOUBLE EGG CUPS, 1939
Lu-Ray Pastels, U.S.A.,
for Taylor Smith & Taylor
Ceramic
Set of five
Price in 1948: $0.65 each
Collection of Elliot T. Fishman

BABY FEEDING CUP, c. 1940
Eva Zeisel
Glazed earthenware
3 x 4 x 3 in.
Brooklyn Museum of Art;
Gift of Eva Zeisel

BABY DISH, c. 1940
Eva Zeisel
Glazed earthenware
2 x 8½ x 7¾ in.
Brooklyn Museum of Art;
Gift of Eva Zeisel

VASE, mid 20th century
Arthur Eugene Baggs, for Marblehead Pottery
Thrown and glazed red earthenware
9¼ x 6¾ in.
The Arthur E. Baggs Memorial Library
Collection, The Ohio State University

Vase, 1942
Arthur Eugene Baggs
Glazed porcelain
8 x 6 in.
The Arthur E. Baggs Memorial Library
Collection, The Ohio State University

***Museum* Dinner Service**, 1942–1945
Eva Zeisel, for Castleton China Company,
New Castle, PA, for the Museum of Modern Art
Glazed, undecorated porcelain
Dinner plate, salad plate, coffee pot with lid,
and coffee cup with saucer
The Arthur E. Baggs Memorial Library
Collection, The Ohio State University

***Lifetime* Ware**, 1947
Jon Hedu, for The Watertown Manufacturing
Company
Melamine
Dinner plate, luncheon plate, butter plate,
fruit saucer, cereal bowl, and cup with saucer
The Museum of Modern Art, New York;
Gift of George E. Weigl Co.

Reagan Service for the White House, 1981
Lenox China
Fine china with scarlet red
and 24 karat gold banding
Service plate, dinner plate, fish/luncheon plate,
dessert plate, salad plate, finger bowl plate,
butter plate, soup bowl, salad/dessert/cereal
bowl, fruit bowl, ramekin, cocktail cup, cream
soup, stand for cream soup bowl, bouillon cup,
stand for bouillon cup, tea cup, saucer, two large
oval platters, buffet round plate, demitasse cup,
saucer for demitasse, and mug
Lenox China Archives, Lenox Brands

Antonelli, Paola. *Mutant Materials in Contemporary Design.* New York: The Museum of Modern Art, 1995.

Attfield, Judy and Pat Kirkham, eds. *A View from the Interior: Feminism, Women, and Design.* London: The Women's Press Lmtd., 1989.

Aynsley, Jeremy. *Nationalism and Internationalism.* London: Victorian and Albert Museum, 1993.

Barquist, David L. *American Tables and Looking Glasses in the Mabel Brady Garvan and Other Collections at Yale University.* New Haven and London: Yale University Press, 1992.

Bowman, Leslie Greene. *American Arts & Crafts: Virtue in Design.* Los Angeles: Los Angeles County Museum of Art; Boston: Bulfinch Press/Little, Brown and Company, 1990.

Conrads, Ulrich, ed. *Programs and Manifestos on 20th-Century Architecture.* Michael Bullock, trans. Cambridge, MA: MIT Press, 1970.

Eidelberg, Martin, ed. *Design 1935–1965: What Modern Was: Selections from the Liliane and David M. Stewart Collection.* Montreal: Musée des Arts Décoratifs de Montréal; New York: Harry N. Abrams, Inc., 1991.

Forty, Adrian. *Objects of Desire: Design and Society, 1750–1980.* New York: Pantheon Books, 1986.

Giedion, Siegfried. *Mechanization Takes Command: A Contribution to Anonymous History.* New York: Oxford University Press, 1948.

Gloag, John. *A Social History of Furniture Design.* New York: Crown Publishers Inc., 1966.

Hayden, Dolores. *The Grand Domestic Revolution.* Cambridge, MA, and London: MIT Press, 1981.

Heisinger, Kathryn B. and George H. Marcus, eds. *Design since 1945.* Philadelphia: Philadelphia Museum of Art, 1983.

Heisinger, Kathryn B. and George H. Marcus. *Landmarks of Twentieth-Century Design.* New York: Abbeville Press, 1993.

Jones, Owen. *The Grammar of Ornament.* New York: Van Nostrand Reinhold Co., 1982 (originally published, 1856).

Mayhew, Edgar de N. and Minor Myers, Jr. *A Documentary History of American Interiors.* New York: Charles Scribner's Sons, 1980.

Pulos, Arthur J. *American Design Ethic.* Cambridge, MA: MIT Press, 1983.

Scully, Vincent J. Jr. *The Shingle Style and the Stick Style,* rev. ed. New Haven and London: Yale University Press, 1971.

Woodham, Jonathan M. *Twentieth-Century Ornament.* New York: Rizzoli, 1990.

Yelavich, Susan. *Design for Life: Our Daily Lives, the Spaces We Shape, and the Ways We Communicate.* New York: Cooper-Hewitt, National Design Museum, Smithsonian Institution and Rizzoli, 1997.

ACKNOWLEDGMENTS

In one of the final scenes of *Citizen Kane*, Orson Welles pitches a high dolly shot of the spoils of a life of collecting: half-opened crates of forgotten acquisitions, objects as the failed hedge against time and solitude. Exploring this cache of things, reporters attempt to find Kane, to excavate his imagined life. Assembling the work in this exhibition has been a bit like walking through a collective attic, though inventories of objects, piled and stored in every available space, secreted in trussed roofs, behind period room displays, in trailers and offsite warehouses. It has made for a fascinating exploration of American material culture of the past two hundred years. During the research and process of assembling the show many individuals have lent invaluable support.

I would like to thank first the lenders to the exhibition, who have been exceptionally informative and helpful. At the Museum of Fine Arts, Boston, I received gracious cooperation and assistance from Jonathan L. Fairbanks, Curator of American Decorative Arts and Sculpture; Anne Moffett, Department Assistant, American Decorative Arts; and Kim Pasko, Registrar. Equally informative and courteous were Barry Harwood, Associate Curator of Decorative Arts; Dianne Fane, Curator of Decorative Arts; Robert Thill, Assistant Curator of Decorative Arts; Elizabeth Reynolds, Registrar; and Lisa Cain, Assistant Registrar, at the Brooklyn Museum of Art.

Henry J. Prebys, Curator of Decorative Arts at the Henry Ford Museum & Greenfield Village, provided an entrée into that collection's vast holdings, especially the archive of Herman Miller furniture; thanks also go to Terry Beamsley, Registrar, and Judith Endelman, Director of Historic Resources. Terrence Riley, Chief Curator of Architecture and Design at The Museum of Modern Art, New York, has been a not infrequent collaborator on varied projects for the Wexner Center. As always, he has my sincere gratitude. This time, I also thank Paola Antonelli, Associate Curator of Architecture and Design, for her helpful discussions, as well as Luisa Lorch, Department of Architecture and Design. At the Musée des Arts Décoratifs de Montréal, I enjoyed the assistance of Diane Charbonneau, Head of Collections Management, and Anne-Marie Chevrier, Cataloguer, Collections Management.

Ellen Denker, Curatorial Consultant at the Lenox Museum of Ceramic Art, offered witty insight along with technical assistance and a close reading of the texts on ceramics. At Knoll, Al Pfeiffer, AIA, has been invaluable in tracking down pieces and providing historical background on the company's role in the evolution of American design; Scott Slankard and Larry Fuhs, Sales Representatives, provided innumerable cut sheets. At Judd Furniture and the Donald Judd Estate, I thank Madeleine Hoffmann and Maiya Keck respectively.

Special thanks are owed to Mary Jo Bole, Associate Professor in Ohio State's Department of Art, for her excitement about this project, suggestions of work to be reviewed, assistance with the Arthur E. Baggs Memorial Library Collection, and ideas about coordination with broader programming for the National Council on Education for the Ceramic Arts (NCECA) conference held in Columbus during the exhibition. Laura Bidwa, NCECA Planning Assistant, and Prudence Gill, Curator of the College of the Arts' Hopkins Hall Gallery, also shared thoughts about coordination with the NCECA meetings.

Individual lenders have given me access to their homes and offices, allowing me to temporarily remove tables, vases, and egg cups still in use there. For their generous cooperation, I thank Dale Abrams, Elliot T. Fishman, Tom and Marian McCollough, and Steve M. Shellabarger. Liz Bank, who shared her extensive knowledge of the profile of Columbus collecting, and Stephen Schwartz also merit thanks. Individual designers and manufacturers have lent additional support: David Khouri, Designer, Comma; Karim Rashid, Designer, and Aldeo Serafini of Curvet USA, Inc.; John Randolph and Bruce Tomb, Partners, of Interim Office of Architecture (IOOA); Ali Tayar, Designer, of Parallel Design Partnership; Julie Cantor of USDA representing Daven Joy and Trav Ebling, Designers, Park Furniture; and Richard Schultz.

In addition to her assistance at The Museum of Modern Art, Paola Antonelli has contributed an enlightening and informative essay to this catalogue, and she has my deep appreciation for her cooperation in this regard. Thanks are also due to all of the participants in the artists' folio section of the volume and to those who assisted them, including Marion Billings for Martin Scorcese, Kristine Helm for Ann Hamilton, Sperone Westwater for Guillermo Kuitca, Janet Borden Inc. for Tina Barney, P.P.O.W. for Lynn Cohen, and Renee Piechocki of Acconci Studio for Vito Acconci. Juan Du and David Yocum helped with Mack Scogin and Merrill Elam's folio page and other materials from Scogin Elam and Bray Architects, Inc.

Beyond the lenders to the exhibition and the participants in the catalogue, staff members at many institutions provided information and insight in the framing of the show. At the Cooper-Hewitt, I thank Susan Yelavich, Associate Director, and Maria Ann Conelli, Chair of the Masters Program in the History of Decorative Arts, for good conversations about material culture and its relation to readings of history, as well as Deborah Shinn, Applied Arts and Industrial Design. Patricia Kane, Curator of American Decorative Arts, at the Yale University Art Gallery provided an early walk through the remarkable collection of American tables on display and in a densely stacked storage facility.

Others who have been generous with their time and expertise include Sarah Nichols, Curator of Decorative Arts, Elizabeth Argo, Curatorial Assistant, and Jennifer Kersting, Decorative and Fine Arts Assistant, at the Carnegie Museum of Art, Pittsburgh; Henry Hawley, Curator of Decorative Arts, and Ann C. Boger at the Cleveland Museum of Art; Kathy Hiesinger, Curator of European Decorative Arts after 1700, Donna Corbin, Assistant Curator of European Decorative Arts, and Diane Minnite, Administrative and Research Assistant, at the Philadelphia Museum of Art; Ulysses G. Dietz, Curator of Decorative Arts, at the Newark Museum; and Margaret Carney, Ph.D., Director of The International Museum of Ceramic Art at Alfred University.

Assistance with research materials and images has also come from Andy Hope, Designer at Co-Motion Design; Robert Viol, Corporate Archivist at Herman Miller Inc.; Amy Howe of The Isamu Noguchi Foundation, Inc.; Ms. Rebecca Rizzo, Promotions at McKenzie Childs; Paul Miller, Curator at the Preservation Society of Newport County; Josh Tenenbaum of the Reagan Library; Erin Budis, Curator of the Shaker Museum and Library; and Betty Monkman, Curator, Lidia Tetrick, Curator, and Harmony Haskins, Photography, at the White House.

At the Wexner Center, this exhibition and publication would have been impossible without the assistance of Maria Kalinke, Graduate Associate in architecture, who has contributed to every phase of the project. William Prince, her predecessor, assisted with the preliminary research. Bill Horrigan, Curator of Media Arts, gave a careful reading to my own essay. Patricia Trumps, Director of Education, and her colleagues on the Wexner Center's education staff, developed a stimulating slate of lectures and other programs related to the exhibition. Graphic Designer Jeff Packard and Editor Ann Bremner, ably aided by Senior Graphic Designer M. Christopher Jones and Assistant Editor Nadine Bailey, shaped the catalogue materials into this handsome volume. I also thank my colleagues in the Wexner Center's exhibitions department for their interest and assistance in the realization of this project. David Bamber, Assistant Exhibition Designer, and Aida Stanish, Graduate Associate in the registrar's office, answered the challenges of installation and transportation logistics. Jill Davis, Exhibitions Coordinator, and Ellen Bethany Napier, Curatorial Assistant, provided guidance and assistance on many details. I am greatful to Donna De Salvo, Curator at Large, for the intellectual depth and rigor that she has given to the overall framing of the collections series. I also thank Sarah J. Rogers, Director of Exhibitions, and Sherri Geldin, Director, for their long-term support and enthusiasm for *On the Table*.

Finally, I add my own note of appreciation to Sherri's in thanking those who have provided financial and promotional support for the exhibition: Chuck and Joyce Shenk, whose generosity has made the *Succession of Collections* exhibition series possible; the Ohio Arts Council; WBNS-TV; and the Wexner Center Foundation.

Mark Robbins
CURATOR OF ARCHITECTURE
WEXNER CENTER FOR THE ARTS

PHOTO AND REPRODUCTION CREDITS

In most instances, photographs of works in the exhibition have been provided by the institution or individual that owns the work. Additional photo and illustration sources and credits are noted in the list below.

p. 6: photo Doug Carr.

pp. 12 and 20: Lucy Staley, *New Trends in Table Settings...and Period Designs, Too* (New York: Hearthside Press Inc., 1968), pl. XIII and p. 137.

p. 15: photo courtesy of The Preservation Society of Newport County.

p. 17: photo Charles Eames Office; *The Herman Miller Collection* (catalogue), 1952, reprinted in Leslie Piña, *Herman Miller: Interior Views* (Atglen, PA: Schiffer Publishing Ltd., 1995), p. 217; reproduced courtesy of Herman Miller Inc.

p. 22: photo Morley Baer; courtesy of Knoll, Inc.

p. 25: Catherine E. Beecher and Harriet Beecher Stowe, *The American Woman's Home* (Hartford, CT: Stowe-Day Foundation, 1975; originally published by J. B. Ford & Co., 1869), fig. 13, p. 34.

p. 27: The Museum of Modern Art, *Machine Art*, sixtieth-anniversary edition (New York: The Museum of Modern Art, 1994; originally published in 1934).

p. 32: photo ©1996 Robert Benson.

p. 50 (right): photo Gino Gareza.

p. 51: photo ©Inter IKEA Systems B.V.

p. 55: photo courtesy of The Isamu Noguchi Foundation, Inc.

p. 56: photo ©1998 The Museum of Modern Art, New York.

p. 59: photo courtesy of Knoll, Inc.

p. 63: photo courtesy of Knoll, Inc.

p. 64: photo David Sundberg.

p. 67: photo Richard K. Loesch.

p. 68: photo ©1998 The Museum of Modern Art, New York.

p. 69: photo courtesy of the Ronald Reagan Library.

pp. 71–73: photos Richard K. Loesch.

pp. 75–76: photos Mary Jo Bole, Rebecca Harvey, Steven Thurston, and Berry von Boekel.

p. 80: photo ©Timothy Hursley.

p. 89: photo Wayne McCall.

p. 95: photos Vito Acconci.

p. 97: photos Scogin Elam and Bray Architects, Inc.

p. 128: *The Herman Miller Collection* (catalogue), 1950, reprinted in Leslie Piña, *Herman Miller: Interior Views* (Atglen, PA: Schiffer Publishing Ltd., 1995), p. 185; reproduced courtesy of Herman Miller Inc.

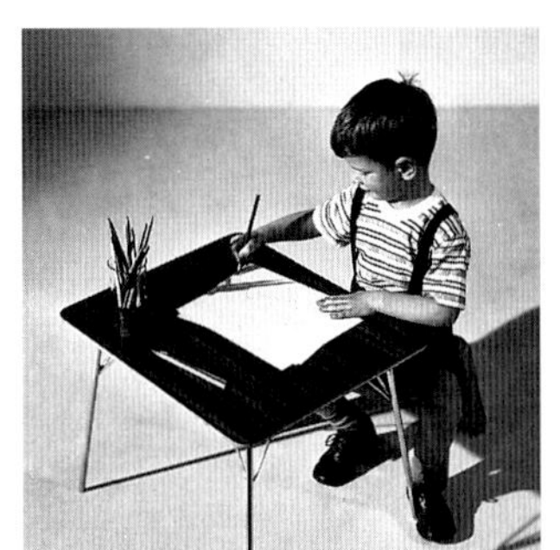

END TABLE